How to Live in Denmark

A humorous guide for foreigners and their Danish friends

Edition 2017

Kay Xander Mellish

ISBN 9788771882964

Publisher: BoD - Copenhagen, Denmark
Printing: BoD - Norderstedt, Germany

CONTENTS

PREFACE: SO, WHAT ARE YOU DOING IN DENMARK?

When I went to my first business meeting in Denmark, I looked around and realized everyone at the table but me had blue eyes.

Denmark is a monoculture, even now, when between 5% and 10% of its residents are not of Danish ethnic origin. People born in Denmark enter state-financed day care institutions when they are about a year old, which is the start of a lifetime controlled chain of events.

Their personalities are formed by universal day care, common-curriculum schools, and publicly-funded after-school clubs, by community beliefs and unspoken expectations about how people should behave and what they should value.

For foreigners, even Danish-looking foreigners, living in Denmark can be like playing a game where everyone knows the rules except you.

Danes generally cut foreigners a lot of slack. They know foreigners are different, not part of the Danish tribe, although on some level they suspect that their non-Danish customs are a bit *mærkelig* – weird – and in some ways backward and wrong. For all their outward humility, most Danes are inwardly convinced that they have the best, most compassionate, most sensible, and most advanced society in the world.

A SOCIETY BASED ON TRUST

Last winter, at around 7 o'clock on a dark evening in Copenhagen, I went to my local train stop on my way to pick up my daughter from a party. Outside the station, I found a little boy crying. Not so little, actually – he was about ten years old, with a crisp new haircut in his light blond hair.

The boy, who said his name was Mike, told me he'd just come back from a friend's house and discovered he couldn't find his way home in the dark. He knew his address, though, and asked if I would walk him home. Apparently, his mother had told him that if he ever got lost, he should just 'ask a lady' to help him out.

So Mike and I walked home, through the urban darkness. He didn't really know his address after all – he just had a general idea of where he lived – so we went up streets and around corners for a while and, having been a New Yorker, I briefly wondered if I was being lead into a trap. But then Mike found his front door and cheerfully bounced through it without really saying goodbye. He was happily and safely home again, having been taught he could trust any random lady he met, even an American on a train platform.

Denmark is a society based on trust, and this is one of the great barriers for newcomers in 'fitting in' here. Danes don't know if they can trust you. They don't know if you will follow the rules they have silently agreed on.

Getting to know the Danes takes time, and to people they do not know, Danes can be closed and sometimes rude. Danes talk to their friends; they don't chat with strangers. Once you do get to know them, Danes are kind, gentle, and loyal.

WHY ARE YOU HERE?

Having lived here since 2000, I've been lucky enough to make some wonderful friends and integrate to the extent a foreigner can in Danish society; my daughter was born here in 2004 and attends a Danish school. Still, I am asked at every Danish dinner party, 'How did you come to Denmark? Why did you come to Denmark? What type of culture shock did you experience once you got here?'

I don't mind answering these questions – particularly if the alternative is to discuss people's home renovations and travel plans, which are the other things that get talked about at Danish dinner parties.

But I didn't really have a lot of culture shock.

First of all, I grew up in Wisconsin, one of the most Scandinavian parts of the United States. Wisconsin is a state with about five and a half million people, the same as Denmark, mostly rural, like Denmark, and with two main cities – an academic one, Madison, the size of Aarhus, and a commercial one, Milwaukee, almost exactly the size of Copenhagen. And it saw massive German, Polish, and Scandinavian immigration about 100 to 150 years ago. You still see a lot of remnants of those European cultures in Wisconsin. People don't change that quickly.

I left Wisconsin when I was 18 to attend New York University, where I had the advantage of living in downtown Manhattan for four years and meeting a lot of fun, creative people who are still friends today. After graduating, I couldn't find a job with my journalism degree, so I took a German class in Berlin and stayed there to work as a freelance reporter for various foreign publications. Later, I moved to Hong Kong and worked for the South China Morning Post for a couple of years; returning to Manhattan, I was on the staff of Dow Jones' old wire services supplying the Wall Street Journal.

By 1999, I was tired of the frenetic pace of New York City and ready to live someplace else. I came to Copenhagen on vacation in 1999 and liked it. After returning to New York, I used the Internet – a relatively new innovation at the time – to find a job in Denmark. When I found one and announced my intention to move, I was met with derision. "You're running away from your problems," said my doctor. "You'll be back within the year," said a guy I was dating at the time.

Fourteen years later, I'm still here, although not without some bumps and bruises. The company that brought me over – furniture and all – collapsed shortly after I arrived, and while I managed to find another job at a similar digital agency, it also went bankrupt as the first internet bubble burst. After nearly a year of unemployment, during which I ate a lot of spaghetti, I found a communications job with Danske Bank, Denmark's largest financial institution.

Danske Bank hasn't gone bankrupt, although it came pretty close during the financial crisis that began in 2008. I left the bank during the crisis and spent a couple of years working for Carlsberg, Denmark's famous beer exporter, before starting my own communications company KXMGroup. It helps Danish companies communicate in English, offering communications coaching, copywriting, translation, and English-language video voiceovers.

I like Denmark; I have no plans to live anywhere else.

THE HOW TO LIVE IN DENMARK PODCAST

In the summer of 2013, I started the How To Live in Denmark podcast, partly to practice my pronunciation and sound techniques, since I record my own video voiceovers. But the podcast has also become a form of service, a way to share what I've learned with other new arrivals. There are a lot of newcomers at the moment, with Southern Europe's economies in disarray, and a constant inflow of bright people from China, India, Pakistan and the Middle East.

Those of you who have followed the How To Live in Denmark podcast may notice a few of the podcasts missing from the book. There was some judicious editing involved to eliminate repetition – for example, I found I had produced three podcasts about the miseries of the long Danish winter.

When I arrived in Denmark, there were several books I found useful, including the multi-author *The Xenophobe's Guide to the Danes*, Morten Strange's *Culture Shock Denmark* (although Morten Strange, a Dane, ultimately left the country for Singapore) and Monica Redlich's *Danish Delight,* first issued in 1939. Each book was a creature of its time, as is this book, which I'm sure will seem outdated within a few years. Denmark is changing quickly.

Nevertheless, I hope it is as helpful to you as these other writers were to me.

Kay Xander Mellish
Copenhagen, July 2014

NOTE ON THE UPDATED EDITION

In the four years since I began working on the *How to Live in Denmark* podcast, Denmark has had a moment in the global spotlight – as both hero and villain.

The heroic Denmark is "the happiest country in the world", the place with the Scandinavian welfare system that keeps everyone safe and secure.

Lifestyle magazines run lavish photo layouts about Danish *hygge*, which they interpret as "sitting home in thick socks surrounded by fancy candles". (The candles can usually be purchased at a fancy price in the magazine's online shop.)

Meanwhile, the Danish style of parenting has been the source of several successful books by female authors – oddly, male authors never seem to write about this.

Even Danish cooking has had a moment, with worldwide enthusiasm for the beets, cabbage and meatballs that make up Nordic cuisine.

WELCOME! NOW PLEASE LEAVE

But Denmark has been a villain, too. It was criticized for being less than welcoming during the European refugee crisis – it even took out ads in Arabic-language newspapers telling people not to come here – and its approach to the foreigners who already live here has been confusing and contradictory.

Danish immigration policies seem designed to welcome people one minute and drive them out the next.

Since the first edition of this book was published, the waiting time to be considered for a permanent residency has gone from 5 to 6 to 8 years, even for someone with a full-time job paying hefty Danish taxes. Citizenship is even harder: you can be disqualified from Danish citizenship for any fine of 3000 kroner or over. 3000 kroner is precisely the cost of a single speeding ticket.

Denmark needs foreigners. Essential industries from architecture to engineering to agriculture to hotels couldn't run without them, and many of the brightest students at Danish universities come from abroad.

At the same time, there's no point in pretending that everyone comes to Denmark with good intentions. In 2016, 75% of the people who appeared in criminal court in Copenhagen had foreign passports; that was actually down from 78% the previous year.

The Danish Finance Ministry went so far as to make a breakdown of which foreigners were profitable for the country (British citizens came out tops) and which were a troublesome expense.

At any rate, this book is dedicated to the many foreigners working to make Denmark strong and prosperous, and to the many good and kind people from around the world who want to know how to live in Denmark.

Kay Xander Mellish
April 2017

DANISH SUMMER

WHY YOU SHOULD RUN OUTSIDE RIGHT NOW

When I first arrived in Denmark during the summer – summer 2000, for those who are counting – one of the things I immediately liked about it was that there was no air conditioning. I had spent the past ten years working in tower blocks in Manhattan, where you are hit by an icy blast of air as you enter on a sunny June day, and with an oven-like blanket of heat when you exit.

In Copenhagen, the summer air is the same inside as it is outside, except perhaps a bit stuffier, what with Danish ventilation technology being somewhat less advanced than Danish heating technology.

That summer of 2000 was a good education in Danish summers, since the sunny weather never actually turned up. In June, it was rainy and cold, and people told me it would probably get better in July. In July, the weather was also poor, but the Danes told me you could generally count on August. August came, grey and drizzling, and people started extolling the general glory of September. And so on. I believe there was some sunshine around Christmas of that year.

Despite the unreliability of summer, there are some well-known Danish summer signifiers. One of them is *sommersild*, which translates to 'summer herring.' There is indeed a lunchtime casserole called summer herring, but that's not what I'm talking about now.

'Summer herring' is a Danish media term for a feature in which attractive young women on the beach or at a local park are photographed wearing not very much clothing as part of a news story.

The news story is generally pretty thin: this year, I have seen summer herring presented with the shocking news that ice cream bars cost more in corner stores than in supermarkets. This was illustrated by some close-up photos of the ice cream bars and girls in bikini tops enjoying them.

You could certainly get angry about this objectification of women. Alternately, you could spare some sympathy for Danish men, whose observation of the female form is limited to parka and sweater-watching for eleven months of every year. (In 2000, all 12 months of the year.)

BEACH LIONS

There is also a male version of 'summer herring.' It's called *strandløver*, or 'beach lions,' usually muscular blond types, although muscular immigrants are also represented. Beach lions don't appear in the media quite as much, and they don't test out ice cream bars, except maybe in publications directed at an all-male audience.

Anyway, even if the weather is bad during the summer, I still always enjoy a trip to Tivoli, the 150-year-old amusement park in downtown Copenhagen.

Tivoli has it all – roller coasters, rock bands, pretty gardens, and most of all great people-watching. If I'm still in Denmark as an old lady, I plan to get a season pass and spend all day sitting on a bench watching the awkward teenaged lovers, joyful families, panicked single dads, and pretty children with their parents' telephone numbers written on their arms in case they wander off. The restaurants in Tivoli are wildly overpriced, but you can bring your own food and have a picnic.

The fruit in Denmark is very good during the summer – fresh red strawberries in June, cherries in July, and wild blackberries in August. Even in downtown Copenhagen, you can still sometimes pick blackberries off the bushes by the subway tracks. Eat them with *crème fraiche*, or as a companion to *koldskål*, the curious buttermilk dish that appears next to the milk cartons in Danish supermarkets the summer.

And, as always with Danish summers, I suggest you run outside as soon as you see the sun shining. You never know how long it's going to last. There's always the chance you might not see it until next year – or, in the case of the summer of 2000, not even then.

NAKED BUT PRIVATE

WHY YOUR DANISH NEIGHBORS WON'T TALK TO YOU

Shortly before I arrived in Denmark in 2000, one of the famous guards outside the Queen's palace at Amalienborg was fired. You've seen these Royal Life Guards on postcards: they're dressed like the British palace guards, only with dark blue coats instead of red. They have the same tall, black, bearskin hats. It's no big secret that being in the Royal Life Guards is an excellent path to a powerful future in corporate Denmark.

Anyway, the guard who was fired was special. She was the first woman to guard the Royal Palace at Amalienborg. There was a lot written about it in the newspapers at the time. Unfortunately, this young lady also had a part-time job. She was a prostitute. She would guard the palace by day and run her business out of the royal barracks in the evening. She found customers via escort ads in the local newspapers.

So, the young lady was fired. But she was not fired because she was a prostitute. She was fired because she'd been ordered by her commander to stop moonlighting, and she did not stop. In fact, she'd been asking her soldier colleagues to drive her to her various nighttime appointments. She was fired for not following orders.

The Danes I talked to didn't find this case particularly shocking.

"It's her private time, when she's not at work," they told me. "She can do whatever she wants in her free time."

That was my introduction to the Danes' passion for privacy and protecting their private lives.

The Danish word *privat* is used a lot. You'll hear Danes talking about their 'private economy,' which means their personal finances. Two of your colleagues may say that they 'know each other privately,' which does not mean they've seen each other without underwear. It just means they get together on weekends.

Where this relates to you as a foreigner is when the Danes around you – your colleagues, your neighbors, the people sitting next to you on the Copenhagen metro - don't want to invade your privacy. This is why they're not talking to you.

Now, let's say I, as an American, saw an African family move into my apartment building. I would think that was pretty interesting. I'd probably want to chat with them about where in Africa they came from and what they were doing in Denmark. Maybe bring them some American cookies and see if I could get invited for a meal to taste some food from their country.

Many Danes would not chat with the African family at all. This is because they are protecting the African family's privacy. Perhaps the family doesn't want to talk. Perhaps they have a secret. In Danish eyes, it can be good manners not to disturb them or ask too many questions. The African family might, from their perspective, see this as Danish unfriendliness.

Danes are cautious about new friendships; they take friendship seriously, seeing it as a lifetime commitment, and don't want to start anything they can't finish.

WHY I GOOGLE MY NEIGHBORS

I do not know most of my neighbors in Denmark. When they move in and out of one of the six apartments in my building, they often don't say hello when they move in or goodbye when they move out.

I will admit here that I have resorted to Googling my neighbors to find out who they are and why they might be using a chainsaw at 10pm on a Saturday night.

Now, you may see some irony here. You may wonder how people who appear half-nude in daily newspapers keep anything private at all.

Well, there are some things that are private in Denmark, and some things that are not.

For example, age. In New York, where I used to live, you didn't ask women their age. And if you did, you'd probably be lied to. I used to take off five or six years, because everyone would assume I was taking off five or six years. If I told my real age, they would have I was assumed I was five or six years older.

In Denmark, everyone knows your age. It's part of your CPR number, which you use for every contact with the government, even checking out library books. If you call to set up an appointment with your doctor, you'll need to give that number, which includes your birth date. Your age is not private in Denmark.

On the other hand, your personal choices are very private. When I lived in Hong Kong, local Chinese people I had just been introduced to would ask me, "Why aren't you married? Don't you want children? You're getting awfully old."

That's not the kind of stuff people in Denmark want to discuss with strangers. They also don't do much office gossip, about who is sleeping with whom, or who is cheating on his or her spouse. That's considered private.

And some things are private because they are considered embarrassing. Like ambition.

Ambition is embarrassing in Denmark. It suggests that you want to be better than someone else.

In an egalitarian society, that's very bad manners. A recent survey showed that 68% of Danes are not interested in being promoted at work. Maybe that's because if you get promoted, whatever additional income you get mostly goes to taxes.

But maybe it's because some Danes were too embarrassed to tell the survey taker that they wanted to get ahead. Ambition is private in Denmark.

Religion is another thing that is very private in Denmark. Even though Denmark is officially a Christian country, and the Queen is head of the state church, to be openly Christian and talk about Jesus or being saved is considered bad manners. It will make most Danish people very uncomfortable. Many Danes see religion as sort of a security blanket for backward, uneducated people, a bit like believing in ghosts. This is one of the many reasons Danes have so much trouble understanding their Muslim minority.

Speaking of religion, my Danish friends have a lot of contempt for the Bible Belt in the U.S., where people loudly declare their religious fervor, and if you're, say, gay, you're expected to hide it, keep it to yourself.

In Denmark, if you're gay, you can tell everybody – but if you're religious, particularly deeply religious, you're expected to hide it, keep it to yourself. That kind of thing is private.

DANISH NAMES

I got a nice note this week from one of my podcast listeners, a fellow named Ole. Now I've never met Ole, and I don't know anything about him except that he sent me a pleasant note. But I can make a guess about him, based on his name, that he is over sixty years of age.

Danish names are very strongly stratified by age. Ole and Finn and Knud and Kaj and Jørn and Jørgen and Poul and Per are all likely to be over sixty, probably over seventy. Their wives and sisters and secret lovers are often named Inge, Karin, or Kirsten.

Or Bente. Bente is a guaranteed old lady's name; there are no young Bentes. There are also no young men named Bent, the male version of the name.

Being named Bent is a problem for Danes who travel because in many English-speaking countries, 'bent' is old-fashioned slang for 'gay.' In those countries, if you hold out your hand and say, "Hi, I'm Bent," you may get an unexpected reaction.

I knew a Danish executive named Bent who was once sent to work in the UK. While he was there, he called himself Ben – no 't.' He even had 'Ben' put on his business cards.

At any rate, it's good to know the general layout of the Danish name curve if you're going to have a job interview or a meeting, because you can get an idea of who's going to be on the other side of the table.

If it's Søren or Mette you're going to meet with, it's someone mid-career, probably in their forties. Søren, Mette, Pia, Rikke, Trine, Pernille, Lars, Jesper, Steen, Kim – these are the middle-aged, middle-management names of Denmark today.

They're the names of my generation.

When I first came to Denmark, I used to joke that you could get into any party by saying, "*Yeah, I'm a good friend of Mette,*" because there was always a Mette in there somewhere.

On the other hand, if you're supposed to meet with Rasmus or Sofie or Maja or Magnus, you're probably going to be talking to someone who might be younger, and quite possibly smarter, than you are. These are names for Danish people in their twenties and early thirties.

In the generation after that, girls are named Mathilde, Sofia, Emma, and Alma; the boys are Albert, Bertil, Louis, or Anton. And there is already a new generation of names coming up behind them: these days the hippest names to give Danish babies are very old-fashioned Viking names. Valdemar. Freja. Holger.

Holger Danske is a legendary figure who is supposed to arise from the grave and save Denmark in its difficult moments. The next Holger Danske may be located in your local kindergarten right now, dribbling organic carrots onto his t-shirt.

THE SHAME OF ANGLICIZED FIRST NAMES

Names go in and out of fashion in every country, and they often tell you even more about a person. In the United States, where I come from, you can make a safe bet that Cody will be white and LaShawn will be black. In Denmark, you can pick out the Muslim names, but otherwise there's not that much cultural distinction.

With one big exception. During the 1960s, there was a fashion for working-class families to use Anglicized names for boys. Tommy. Jimmy. Johnny. Dennis. Alan. Kenneth. Some of these kids grew up to be fine members of society, but others grew up to be troublemakers. The names still carry a slight frisson of 'loser' around them: a friend of that age once told me a story about a teacher who started the school year by saying, "Okay, all you guys with a 'y' at the end of your names – I don't want any smart-ass behavior from you guys this year!"

The sad thing, said my friend, was that the teacher was pretty much on target when it came to the problem children.

The guys who have it toughest are named Brian – or Breean, as the Danes say it. Bree-an has become a slang term for a 'lunkheaded working-class guy.' *Ah...he's such a Brian.*

So, if you meet a successful man named Brian, or Kenny, or Tonny (which is the Danish version of Tony), this is a man who has worked hard to overcome his background and the disadvantage of what, to the Danes, is a very unfortunate first name.

PAINFUL HUGS AND POISON GIFTS

WHEN THE SAME WORDS MEAN DIFFERENT THINGS IN DANISH AND ENGLISH

When you're just starting to learn Danish, some people may tell you that Danish and English are very much alike.

In some ways, they are. The Vikings invaded England several times and left behind their language as well as their genes.

The Danish word *sky*, meaning cloud, became the English word 'sky.' *Øl* – Danish beer – is 'ale' in English.

But in some ways, English and Danish are not alike, and that can cause problems. Back in the days when I was learning French, they called them 'false friends' – words that look identical but mean entirely different things.

The one I noticed first when I arrived in Denmark was *slut*. *Slut* means 'finished' in Danish, all done, but the same four letters in English spell 'slut,' which is a not very nice name for someone, usually a woman, who is very friendly in a naked sort of way.

When I first arrived, I remember seeing magazines with a name and a face on the cover, and it would say in big letters 'SLUT!'

I thought, wow, that's harsh. That's a nasty thing to call that poor lady. But, of course, in Danish, it was just saying *slut*. That lady was finished with something – with her relationship, or her TV show, or her handball tournament. Not 'slut', but *slut*!

Slut! still gets me sometimes, and so does *hug*. A 'hug', in English, is a nice thing you get from your sweetheart or your grandma. But in Danish, a *hug* is a karate chop. If you get a *hug* from someone, it hurts. It's also used as a metaphor – in Danish newspapers, Danish politicians are often getting a *hug* from their political opponents. Nobody wants that kind of hug.

Another one that drives me crazy is *student*. In English, a 'student' is anybody who goes to school, anybody who is learning something. You could be a five-year-old student or an 85-year-old student.

That's not true in Danish. A *student* is someone who has finished studying, or has at least just finished the big *student* exam that 18-year-olds take before going on to higher education; in the spring, you'll see them around town with their traditional white *student* hats on, and people will say of a young man, "He's just become a *student*!" That means he's just passed that test. You're not a *student* until you pass the test.

This goes on and on. The English word 'gift', like a birthday present, is *gift* in Danish. Poison. So, if you see a package with the word *gift* and a skull and crossbones, it doesn't mean there's been a birthday party for a pirate. *Gift* – poison – will kill you. Coincidentally, *gift* is also the Danish word for getting married.

DANES, DUTCH, DEUTSCHLAND

WHY PEOPLE CONFUSE DENMARK WITH ITS NEIGHBORS

I run my own small business, so often I outsource small tasks. For example, I outsourced the writing of some tweets to promote the *How to Live in Denmark* podcast to Jessie, a college student in the United States. Jessie did a good job, with one major exception: in all one hundred tweets, she confused the word *Danish* with the word *Dutch*.

She wrote: '*Copenhagen Fashion Week – Check out the latest in Dutch fashion.*' '*Stay healthy like the Dutch: Bicycle through Denmark.*' '*Top 10 restaurants in Copenhagen: Enjoy Dutch cuisine.*'

Now, please don't give me that stereotype about geographically dumb Americans. At least not until Europeans can tell me the difference between *Iowa, Idaho,* and *Ohio* – and yes, there is a difference.

The fact is, confusing the Dutch and the Danes is understandable.

They both represent small, peaceful countries with seafaring traditions. Countries that are best known for healthy blond people on bicycles, rushing home to see their monarchs on TV and eat potato-based dishes. The Dutch are known for their beautiful windmills. The Danes are known for their ugly wind turbines. It's an understandable mistake.

But among the neighbors to Denmark, it's actually not the Dutch who resemble the Danes most. It's the Germans. Despite their complicated relationship with the country that occupied them as recently as 1940, Danes are more German than they'd ever want to admit.

For example, the Germans love punctuality – *pünktlichkeit*. So do the Danes.

In Denmark, if you have a business meeting at 10am, you need to show up at precisely 10:00am. 10:03 is not good. 10:05 is embarrassing – you'd better apologize. 10:10 is just not done.

And it's not just business. I've had dinner parties where my guests actually circle the block so they can ring the bell at 8-dot-00-dot-00.

Now, this is not entirely a bad thing. The buses run on time in Denmark. The trains often run on time. Otherwise, mass transit wouldn't be so popular.

Both countries also like order. If a Dane wants to say that someone is a trustworthy guy, they say he's *ordentlig* – orderly. When they want you to clarify something, they ask you to do it 'for the sake of good order.' *For god ordens skyld*. For the sake of good order, let's write this agreement down. Of course, Germans' love of order is legendary.

FIRST NAMES VS. TITLES

That said, Germans value hierarchy in a way Danes do not.

In Denmark, just about everybody uses his or her first name. Third-grade teachers, emergency room doctors, or starchy bank presidents can all be addressed as just 'Mette,' 'Rasmus,' or 'Peter.'

An incredibly old lady might be *Fru Jensen*, but I don't think I've heard the corresponding masculine title, *Herr Jensen*, even once in the 17 years I've been here.

Germans, on the other hand, love their titles, and even pile them on top of each other: *Herr Professor Doktor von Schmidt.* Rank still means something in Germany.

The German language reflects this formality: *Sie*, the formal version of you, is still very much in use in Germany, and woe be it to you if you use *du* when the German you're talking to is expecting *Sie*.

That's not true in Denmark. Everybody is *du*. There is a formal Danish 'you,' *De*, which immigrants still learn in language school, but it is never used in conversation, except with the snobbier members of the royal family. (Crown Prince Frederik, the future king, is reportedly quite happy with *du*, while his pompous younger brother Joachim insists on *De*.)

THE SWEDES AND THEIR HAIRCUTS

The Danes most problematic national relationship is not with the Germans, but with the Swedes, their annoying next door 'big brother.' While Danes are sometimes called the Latins of the North - they know how to open a bottle of wine and enjoy life – the Swedes are often referred to as the Prussians of the North. They're tall. They stand up straight. They're stiff, have a lot of rigid rules they like to follow, and like to lecture others about their failure to live up to what they believe are high-minded Swedish standards.

Danes find that annoying as hell, and take a perverse joy in following the various things that go wrong in Sweden via the

Danish newspapers, which sometimes report on these problems more thoroughly than the Swedish media does. Danes make fun of the Swedish men's haircuts – that terrible two-level 'mullet' haircut that was popular in the 1980s is known in Danish as *Swedish hair*. They also tend to think Swedes can't hold their liquor, a stereotype born of the hoards of drunken football fans who come to Copenhagen to watch games and drink cheap (by Swedish standards) booze.

Swedes, meanwhile, dislike the Danish language, which most of them cannot understand. (The exception is Swedes who grew up in the south of the country watching Danish TV.) Danish sounds sloppy to them, and the Danes themselves seem a little lazy, a bit unpredictable, and most assuredly racist, since they fail to appreciate the superior Swedish standards of multiculturalism.

Maybe both perspectives have a bit of truth to them. There's an old saying that inside every Swede is a little policeman trying to get out … and inside every Dane, there's a little criminal.

DANISH BABIES

ROLLING ROYALTY AND TRIBAL NAMES

Denmark is a small country, and Danish people tend to think small things are good. Small cars. Small homes. Small ambitions when it comes to international team sports. But one thing in Denmark is never small – a baby carriage.

Danes seem to believe that a carriage (or pram) for a new baby should be roughly the size of a hotel room on wheels.

Inside, the baby will be wrapped up warm with a fat feather blanket – even in the summer. There will also be room for pillows, books, toys, snacks, diapers, and extra clothes in the giant baby carriage.

Danish babies are like rolling royalty. Everything they need is at their tiny fingertips.

A BABY LIFE OF PRIVILEGE

Generally, Danish babies live a privileged life. Denmark is a good place to be a baby. The food and the health care situation is good, and Mom gets four weeks at home before you are born and 12 weeks after. Then she and Dad can split the rest of a year of paid leave from work.

Danish parents make good use of this time. It's led to a small industry of baby music classes. Baby swimming. Baby yoga. And baby café meetings.

Someday, you may be sitting in a café in Denmark and suddenly find yourself surrounded by four to six babies and their parents. This is because the Danish government puts together groups of women who live close to each other and all have babies within a few days of each other.

These are called mother's groups – and yes, they still are mostly mothers. They meet, they drink coffee, they discuss diapers and nap times, and then afterwards they all try to get their giant baby carriages onto a single city bus. It's a fight to the finish.

Anyway, if the mother's group has the right chemistry, it can meet for decades. I know a woman whose kid is in his thirties, and she still meets with her mother's group once a year.

WATCH OUT FOR TRIBAL NAMES

Every baby born in Denmark gets an official birth certificate from the nearest church, even if the parents are not Christians. And Danish babies must have a first name that's on the approved list. There's a list of approved names in Denmark, a long list, and it has plenty of Muslim and African names on it, but you can't be like a Hollywood star and name your child 'Pilot Inspektor' – it's against Danish law. You also can't give a boy a girl's name or vice-versa.

And if the baby's other parent is a Dane, you'll find that last names can be a drama as well. Anybody who wants to can be a Hansen or a Nielsen, but there is also a list of last names that are restricted.

Since fewer than 2000 people in Denmark use these last names, they're considered protected 'tribal names' (*slægtnavn*), or bloodline names. Many *slægtnavn* are related to places, particularly the old farm estates from the 18th and 19th century. Only certain members of the family are allowed to use the name, and depending on the baby's place in the family line, you may have to ask some of the older family members for permission. I know a guy whose great-aunt, on her deathbed, gave him permission to use the *slægtnavn*. He was thrilled. It was a big deal.

THE CPR AS THE ENTRANCE CARD
TO THE WELFARE STATE

Babies born in Denmark also get a CPR number right away, which identifies them as a participant in the Danish welfare state. CPR numbers include your birthday plus four additional numbers – even for girls, odd for boys.

Your baby needs a CPR to get on the waiting list for government child care. Child care is not free in Denmark, but it is heavily subsidized by taxes, and 97% of Danish kids go to government-run day care. Even the princes and the princesses of the royal family do. In popular areas like Copenhagen, there can be a long wait for a spot in a *vuggestue*, or cradle room.

The *vuggestue* is where eight-month-old Danes start meeting each other and building the lifelong friendships that make it so hard to meet anybody when you come to Denmark as an adult foreigner.

IT'S ALL ABOUT 'FREE PLAY.'

At *vuggestue*, the program is not very structured. Danes are great believers in what they call free play, which basically involves kids running around and doing whatever they feel like at the moment. Adults generally don't interfere unless the kids are in a life-threatening situation.

Danes don't really do competitive parenting: there's none of this learning violin or learning to speak Mandarin before age 3. I tried to give my daughter piano lessons at age 4 – which she asked for! – and faced a lot of Danish disapproval. *"She should be having free play!"* everybody said. (It was only half an hour a week.)

Anyway, when playtime is done and it's time for a nap, smaller Danish babies sleep outdoors. This old Viking tradition is considered very healthy, and good for their little lungs. If it's raining, babies sleep under an overhang, but if it's just ordinary, cold, grey, Danish weather, they're still out there, even in the winter, strapped into their giant baby carriages. Usually under the same fat feather quilt they wore in the summer and wearing a little hat, warm and comfy, nice and safe.

DANES AND CYCLING

TWO-WHEELED VIKINGS AND WHY I OWN THREE BIKES

In a country where new cars are taxed at 150% – that means a DK100,000 car will cost you DK250,000 – bikes are bound to be popular.

Everybody bikes in Denmark. You'll see executives, male and female, in grey pinstriped business suits on bikes. You'll see people toting their kids around in special bike trailers. You'll see old ladies biking very, very slowly with a lot of people stuck behind them, and you'll see me, trying to balance my newly-collected dry cleaning on my bike because I don't have a car.

The fact that Denmark is relatively flat helps – nobody likes to bike uphill – as does the fact that the climate is temperate. Denmark is as far north as parts of Alaska, but it isn't bitterly cold in the winter. Even in January, you'll see Danish commuters pumping their bikes through the snow. In Copenhagen, the bike lanes get plowed before the streets do.

Most people in Copenhagen have more than one bike, sometimes three. One might be a racing bike or a mountain bike, and the other might be a 'shopper' bike with a big basket for bringing home groceries.

It's also quite common to have an extra, ugly bike. An ugly bike is a bike that gets no love and often no maintenance. It's a rusted, broken-down bike you use for short commutes and to leave at the train station.

When I used to work at Carlsberg, the beer company, I'd take my shopper bike to the train station by my house, get on the train, and then get off at the stop near Carlsberg, where I had another bike waiting – an ugly bike.

It wasn't a great neighborhood, so I needed a not very nice bike, something that wouldn't be worth the effort to steal.

I'd ride the ugly bike to work. At the end of the day, I'd ride the ugly bike back to the station by Carlsberg, leave it there, get back on the train, get off at the stop by my house, and ride my shopper bike home.

Two bikes and a train – that's one way to commute in Denmark. In Copenhagen, it's also common to take your bike on the train with you. There are special train cars these days for bicycles and their riders only: non-cyclists have to sit somewhere else.

THE VIKINGS' LAST STAND

If you want to live in urban Denmark, you will need a bicycle. Bikes are so important that the government actually teaches immigrants how to bike so they can get around.

Apparently, it also teaches the immigrants good bicycle etiquette, because they have much better cycling manners than native-born Danes.

For Danes, bicycle lanes are the Vikings' last stand. Those gentle blond people, those people who will wait two minutes at a red 'don't walk' sign instead of crossing an empty street

– armed with a bike, they turn vicious and brutal. They will scream at you, lecture you, start pointless arguments as you pass each other and then pass each other again in the bicycle lanes. They ring their bicycle bell dozens of times if they think you are holding up their all-important trip to the supermarket.

They also text while they're cycling, talk on the phone while they're cycling, and groove to music through giant head-phones while they're cycling. They go through red lights and intentionally go the wrong way in bicycle lanes. They ride straight down sidewalks, ringing their little bells to tell pedes-trians to get out of the way.

Occasionally, the police in Copenhagen do bicycle raids. They hide around corners and watch Danish bicyclists do all the things they do on a daily basis anyway. Then they hand out tickets for 750 kroner, which must be a nice little money-earn-er for the municipality.

If they could write a ticket every time Danish Viking bicy-clists did something aggressive or illegal, you could cut down on some of those notorious Danish taxes. Think about that, guardians of the welfare state.

DANES AND FASHION

ALL THE COLORS OF THE DANISH LANDSCAPE

I can't remember exactly what the social occasion was, but when I was fairly new to Copenhagen, I met a man who was a refugee from a country in Sub-Saharan Africa. He had escaped his homeland by way of Cairo, Egypt, and ended up in Denmark.

What I do remember is his account of what it was like to come to Copenhagen after living in a busy, colorful city like Cairo. He asked another refugee, a guy who'd been here longer, to show him downtown Copenhagen. The guy drove him to, I don't know, Gammel Strand on a Tuesday night in February, and there was no one there. All the Danes were home enjoying their homes and *hygge*, and the streets were dark and empty. My friend got very angry at the other refugee. Said he'd tricked him. "Where is the city? This is not the city!" he cried out. But it was.

Anyway, I also remember this African refugee's comments about Danish fashion. He said he had trouble shopping here, because Danish clothes all look alike. Every store you go to, it's got the same grey sweater, he said.

Now, that's not entirely true. You could also find a navy blue sweater. I've even seen green sweaters.

Danes dress to match the Danish landscape. That means grey. And brown, and green, and some blue. Maybe some beige for the adventurous.

If you find yourself wearing purple or orange, or hot pink, you will stand out in Denmark. Those colors are only worn by children, or sometimes by middle-aged ladies trying to make a statement.

Now, there is such a thing as Danish fashion, and there is a Danish Fashion Week. Designers like Malene Birger, Bruuns Bazaar, and Day Birger et Mikkelsen have made a name for themselves internationally. But what they design is not what your average Dane wears.

What the average Dane wears is outerwear. It's cold in Denmark, so people's wardrobes are heavy on sweaters, boots, and coats and jackets.

A PLASTIC JOGGING SUIT

There's even a category of outerwear I never knew existed called 'rain gear.' Rain gear is like a plastic jogging suit, and it goes over your clothes and allows you to bicycle or walk around in the rain without getting wet. It's like galoshes for your body. It comes in all the Danish fashion colors – grey, green, blue, and sometimes brown for the gaudy types.

Anyway, if you really do need some color in your life, scarves are very big. When I was growing up in the United States, colorful neck scarves were something worn by the foreign exchange student with the funny name. I never understood why.

Now that I am the foreigner, I do understand. It's cold here, and rooms are not overheated the way they sometimes are in the States. A scarf keeps you from shivering. A scarf saves you from a sore throat. Personally, I now own summer scarves, which are light cotton; fall scarves, which are thin, flat wool; and winter scarves, which are about as thick as a boa constrictor around my neck. On a cold, windy, rainy day, you'll want that boa constrictor.

Speaking of wildlife, Copenhagen recently opened a beautiful new aquarium. It's full of tropical fish in gorgeous tropical colors – hot magenta, lemon yellow, vibrant orange – brought to Denmark from all over the world.

But what many people don't know is that there is another aquarium just north of the city in Helsingor – one full of fish from local waters. It shows brown fish, and beige fish, and slightly grey fish. These are the Danish fish.

A THATCHED ROOF OVER YOUR HEAD

FINDING A PLACE TO LIVE IN DENMARK

Before I moved to Denmark, I didn't know what a thatcher was. Of course, I had heard of Margaret Thatcher, the former British prime minister. But a thatcher – as in a paying job like a carpenter or a massage therapist – was something I was not familiar with.

A thatcher, I now know, is a person who makes a thatched roof. A straw roof, basically. There are thousands of thatched roofs in Denmark, and they're actually very practical for the climate and very environmentally friendly. They keep the heat in and the rain out.

If you want to live in a house with a thatched roof in Denmark, you probably can. A lot of them are vacant because they tend to be located in the countryside, in what's sometimes called the "rotten banana" of slowly dying rural towns.

But as a new arrival to Denmark, you will probably want to live in a city – Copenhagen, Aarhus, Aalborg, or Odense. Maybe Billund if you work for Lego.

The bigger the city, the harder it will be for you to find a place to live. Or at least a reasonably-priced place to rent.

This is because renting is for suckers in Denmark. Danes buy their homes as soon as they can afford a down payment, because they can write the mortgage interest off their giant Danish taxes. Parents often buy their eighteen-year-old children a small apartment as an investment when the kids leave for college. Since university tuition in Denmark is tax-financed, this is a kind of 'goodbye and good luck' present given when it's time for a grown child to get out of the family home.

If you do need to rent, you have two options. Option A: a fabulously designed apartment that looks like a photo layout in a glossy architectural magazine. Option B: a cheap, well-constructed, centrally-located apartment perfectly suited for your needs.

If you want the former – the design apartment – all you have to do is pay about DK15,000 a month, plus a three-month security deposit, plus three months rent in advance. Then you can go ahead and move in your designer furniture, all your beautiful but uncomfortable chairs and your oddly-shaped lamps.

If you want the latter – the cheap, well-constructed, centrally-located apartment perfectly suited for your needs – just get on a waiting list. Wait 20-25 years, and in 2040 or so, you're going to have a fantastic place to live.

Lots of people want cheap apartments in the big cities, and the competition is tough. Many Danes are put on the waiting lists as babies, only to come to the top as they reach adulthood. Sometimes people in desperate need, such as refugees, are allowed to jump the list, but exceptions are rare.

You can look for an apartment on some of the online services connecting landlords and renters; new ones pop up all the time. I am reliably informed that the best way to use them is to be constantly online, and be the first person to call when a new apartment is posted. That said, many online services are also popular with scammers who attempt to take deposits on apartments they do not own.

LIVING ON BORROWED TIME IN A SUBLET

If you've just arrived and are looking for a place, it's common to live in someone else's apartment. If they're still living in the apartment, you're just looking for a room, a *værelse;* if you have the whole place to yourself, it's called a *fremleje*, or sublet.

I did sublets when I first moved to Denmark. The downside of this is that you can get booted out with very little notice. The person working abroad gets fired, the person moving in with a lover breaks up, the person traveling for a year breaks an ankle. Suddenly, you and your suitcases and your beautiful but uncomfortable chairs have a week or so to find someplace else to live.

Getting booted out of a sublet was what finally convinced me to buy a place, which I recommend you do if you plan to be in Denmark for more than a couple of years. You can choose between an *ejerbolig*, in which you own your apartment outright, or *andelsbolig*, in which you own a share of a commonly-owned building. *Andelsboliger* are cheaper, but you have to be prepared to figure out the overall health of the building's finances, which can require a lot of reading in Danish.

Alternately, you could buy a house – think again about those abandoned cottages in the countryside with the thatched roofs. They're a bit of a commute, but no one will ever try to kick you out of them. All you have to do, about once every twenty years, is pay for a visit by the thatcher.

DANISH DESIGN

FROM TEENY-WEENY FANCY GLASSES TO THIEVES THAT STEAL CHAIRS

I moved to Denmark in 2000, but I was actually there briefly in 1984 – for less than one day. It was during my Eurail pass days, and I arrived in the morning from Amsterdam and before taking the night boat to Norway.

It wasn't a good experience. Copenhagen was very different in those days: less prosperous, less open, less social. There were no cafés then, and I had a lot of trouble finding something to eat. I walked and walked and ended up in the coffee shop at the SAS Radisson Hotel, a big 1970s concrete block on Amager.

Anyway, I took only one picture that day, and it was of a toilet at the hotel. It was the most beautifully designed toilet I had ever seen. All round, streamlined corners. It looked like a cross between an egg and a spaceship. I was really impressed. I took a picture.

I didn't know it then, but I'd just seen my first example of local Danish design.

Danes are passionate about design, and they really believe in making everything that is useful also beautiful, even a toilet. After living here a while, you just come to expect it.

What we think of now as Danish design – light, curvy, with a sense of humor – originated after the Second World War. Before that, Danish furniture was heavy, dark, and ponderous. Lots of dark wood, sometimes carved with little figures of cows or farmers. When you visit your Danish friends, you may notice giant pieces of furniture taking up a lot of space in their small urban apartments. These are usually heirlooms from grandparents, mementos of past designs that no one quite has the heart to throw out.

Another type of Grandparent Danish design is the hand-painted Christmas plate from Royal Copenhagen; there's a special one made for each birth year, a common gift to children. The plates are too fancy to be used for eating, so they're usually hung up on the wall instead.

Grandparents and great-grandparents also like teeny-weeny fancy crystal glasses, for drinking shots of *Gammel Dansk* bitter liquor, sometimes for breakfast. And they like porcelain hand-painted figurines of clowns or pretty dancing girls or puppies or rosy-cheeked shepherds. If you like that stuff too, second-hand shops in Denmark have plenty to sell you.

DESIGNER HOUSEWARES, NOT CLOTHES

But anyway, that's old Danish design. New Danish design is minimalist, white, and empty. And there are a few standard elements that show Danish society you have a well-designed home. An Arne Jacobsen chair, for example: the Ant, or the Egg, or the Swan. A PH Lamp, which looks kind of like a metal upside-down wedding cake. A Rosendahl water jug. A silver Georg Jensen fruit bowl. A Kay Bojesen wooden monkey. It's almost like a deck of cards – I've got two swans, an egg, and a monkey. It's a full house!

Ironically, Danes don't care all that much about designer names when it comes to clothes and handbags. I can't remember the last time I saw a Louis Vuitton bag carried in Copenhagen. But when it comes to home design, it's all about the brand name classics. Anyway, give a Dane a choice of fixing up his wardrobe or fixing up his kitchen, and he'll pick the kitchen, every time.

That said, it can be dangerous to have these expensive design items in your home. Thieves target them. Criminal gangs go through the real estate ads to see which houses for sale have expensive designer furniture, and then break in. When I worked at Carlsberg, a Fortune 500 company, someone broke into the headquarters over the weekend – and stole nothing but six Swan chairs in the lobby.

NO PLANNED HANGOVERS

17 YEARS AFTER MOVING TO DENMARK, HERE ARE SOME WAYS I WON'T FIT IN

More than a decade after moving to Denmark, I am pretty well integrated into Danish society. I've learned to speak Danish, I pay my taxes, I bike everywhere, I send my daughter to a Danish school. I enjoy a nice slice of dark rye *rugbrød* – even when I'm on my own and don't have to impress anyone with how healthy I'm eating.

But there are a few ways I simply refuse to integrate. I will not do things the Danish way.

Here's one example: I just won't follow the Danish way of introducing people to each other. Where I come from, if I'm with one friend – let's say, A, Anders, and we run into another friend, let's say B, Bente, I introduce them to each other. I say, "Anders, this is Bente, one of my favorite clients. Bente, Anders is my personal trainer." That way they know a little bit about each other, so we can all participate in the short conversation that follows.

That's not the Danish way. In the Danish way, people are expected to introduce themselves. Anders sticks out his hand and says "Anders." And Bente sticks out her hand and says, "Bente." That's it. And then I chat briefly and uncomfortably with Bente while Anders kind of stands there like one of the bronze statues in Ørsteds Park. Or, worse, stands there while Bente says, "I hear you're looking for a new personal trainer. I know a great guy!"

So, I do try to introduce them to each other, in my American way, and they try to introduce themselves, in the Danish way, and it's all a mess as we talk over each other. I have failed to integrate.

Another way I've failed to integrate is that I don't listen to Danish pop music and I don't watch Danish TV. Now, I know that there are some Danish TV dramas that have become famous all over the world – *Borgen,* for example – but there's also a lot of the usual entertainment filler. Modern Danish TV features the same reality programming you see in any other country – dancing and singing contests, mostly. But Denmark is a small country, with about five and a half million people, and most of them are shy. Trust me when I tell you that there is not that much talent to choose from.

Yet it makes my Danish acquaintances concerned, and sometimes upset, when I say I don't watch their TV. DR, which runs the national radio and TV channels, is seen as a way to kind of bind everyone together. That's why everyone is legally required to pay about $600 a year for it, whether they watch it or not.

If I was going to watch trashy entertainment, I'd watch American trash. God knows we have enough of it.

THE PASSION FOR LICORICE

I have also failed to integrate my diet with the Danish food culture. I don't eat nearly enough pork, and I've yet to master fried fish balls. I don't like herring. And I'm not over the moon about licorice.

Licorice to a Dane is like a chili pepper to a Texan – it is their culinary *ne plus ultra*. In Denmark, you can buy sweet licorice, salt licorice, chocolate-covered licorice, licorice syrup for your coffee, powdered licorice to put on chicken or fish... they are nuts about it. I swear, I think it's something genetic. If you have this specific gene, licorice tastes amazing, like, say, chocolate to everyone else.

In general, Danes eat a lot of candy. They binge eat, and they teach their children to binge eat.

The way we handle candy at my house is that I let my daughter have a little bit of candy or a cookie after school, or perhaps after the evening meal.

Danes don't do this. There is, theoretically, no candy all week, and then a giant bowl of candy on Friday night. Friday candy, it's called, and it's linked to a special Disney show on TV.

They have the same attitude towards alcohol. I'll often have a cocktail at the end of the workday or a glass of wine with dinner. I know my Danish friends think this is a little suspect, and wonder if I secretly may have an alcohol problem.

I don't drink like the Danes. What they do is avoid alcohol all week, and then get absolutely stink-o on the weekend or when they go to a party. Getting stink-o is an expected part of the evening's entertainment. Sometimes I try to make weekend plans with Danish friends and they'll say, "Can't make it! We'll be out the night before, so we'll have a hangover that day." They plan their hangover!

Not drinking, of course, has its advantages: the Monday morning after an office party, I have nothing to regret and no apologies required.

CRIME AND PUNISHMENT IN DENMARK

JUST BUY MORE INSURANCE

A couple of years ago, my daughter buried her mobile phone in the sandbox at school.

She buried her mobile phone deep in the sand, too deep to hear it ring, and then she couldn't find it. She dug and dug, and then she panicked, and she blamed another girl. She said the other girl had buried the phone in the sandbox.

Pretty soon lie piled on top of lie, and we ended up with a Richard Nixon type situation, in which the lies were far worse than the original crime. When we finally unraveled it all, I had to apologize to the other girl's mother.

And I punished my daughter, who was old enough to know better. I took her screens away – her online games and her YouTube access – for a month.

The Danish parents around me were horrified. The idea of punishment, in Danish eyes, is old-fashioned and perhaps a bit criminal in itself. From the Danish point of view, almost all problems can be solved by talking about them.

The Danish parents believed I should have simply spoken strongly to my daughter and explained to her that that it's not

OK to get someone else in trouble, while trying to save your own butt, after doing something colossally stupid. The explanation is the remedy.

By adding a penalty, they believe, I was just being an adult bully.

IT'S OK TO IMPOSE FINES

This doesn't mean there are no penalties in Denmark. The Danes are big on fines. You'll see the controllers prowling the S-trains in Copenhagen, asking to see tickets, and raining down a giant fine on those who don't have them. Even if you have a ticket, but not precisely the correct ticket, you still get the fine. No questions allowed, no pity. (They nab a lot of well-meaning tourists this way, leaving them with a 750 kroner bill as a souvenir.)

You can get a fine for bicycling aggressively, and you get an automatic fine for paying a bill even one day late. And because Denmark is a centralized system based around your CPR number, these fines get added to your taxes or taken away from your government benefits, so there's no avoiding them.

But larger crimes leave Danes at a loss. This is a society built on trust. You see that trust everywhere – coats left on unguarded coat racks, bikes barely locked, children as young as eight or nine taking public transportation alone.

At my post office, people send their expensive packages by putting them into a big open bin. It wouldn't take a very bright or ambitious criminal to just take a couple of promising-looking packages back out again and be on his way.

Danish society is not set up to expect criminal behavior, or to guard against it. When that trust is broken, Danes aren't entirely sure what to do.

Policing in general seems rather passive in Denmark. You'll rarely see police officers in Copenhagen, which is unusual for a big city. You do hear constant announcements on the trains and in train stations that pickpockets are loose.

Criminal gangs have discovered that Denmark is an easy mark. They don't see a society built on trust and respect – they see a lot of unsecured villas in fancy neighborhoods, filled with designer furniture and knick-knacks that are easy to resell.

But the Danish response to crime is, again, not punishment. The classic Danish response is to buy more insurance. You can insure just about anything in Denmark – insure your home against theft, or your bike against theft, or your mobile telephone against theft.

That said, Denmark is still a mostly peaceful place, and the people you really have to fear in Denmark are not the criminals. The people you really have to fear are the tax authorities.

CHEATING ON MOTHER NATURE

DANES AND ENVIRONMENTALISM

Autumn can be beautiful in Denmark. Golden sun and blue skies, red and yellow and orange leaves on the trees. Just gorgeous. Some years, it's unusually warm. It's always exciting when, instead of wearing your winter coat every day from October to April, you can wear it every day from *November* to April.

But this unusually pleasant weather can't help but spark conversation about global warming. So far, the biggest impact climate change has had on Denmark are some severe rainstorms, which end up flooding a lot of basements and overwhelming a lot of sewer systems. It's intriguing to think that plumbers may become the great heroes of the twenty-first century.

Danes care about climate change, and they've made a business specialty of green technology, or what they like to call clean technology. Cleantech. Denmark sells windmills to create wind power, and burns most of its household garbage in an environmentally friendly way to create home heating.

Danes care about the environment because they care about nature. Less than a hundred years ago, Denmark was a mostly agricultural country, and Danes still feel close to the land. Children in Denmark are constantly being taken out into whatever forests or meadows are nearby – in the cities, they get packed onto buses and trains to go get the forest experience. There's even something called forest kindergarten (*skovbørnehave*) for children age 3 to 6. If you go to a forest kindergarten, you're out in the woods every day, rain or shine, hot or cold.

THE WORLD'S FOURTH BIGGEST POLLUTER, PER CAPITA

So, it's ironic, given this romance between Danes and environmentalism, that Denmark was recently named the world's fourth biggest polluter per capita by the World Wildlife Fund. Only three Middle Eastern countries. – Kuwait, Qatar, and the UAE, were worse. (The US was 8th.)

The reason the Danes come in so high on this list is meat, specifically pigs. Pigs and pig products are Denmark's major exports. Live pigs, pork, and diabetic insulin, which is genetically modified based on an extract from the pancreas of pigs. Denmark has more pigs than people; it's the pigs that pay for all Denmark's chic corporate sustainability departments and all those wind turbines.

The modern Danish clean-energy economy is built on the back of pigs, and pigs are environmentally dirty. So are Denmark's thriving dairy industry and wearable fur industry.

What's more, the World Wildlife Fund tracks not only local pollution, but the pollution local consumers produce elsewhere. So, if a Dane buys a T-shirt from H&M or an iPhone that is produced in China, the pollution goes on the Danish account. And Danes buy a lot of stuff from abroad.

Danes also love to eat meat, from both local and international sources. And they love to travel. Airplanes leave a terrible carbon footprint.

Now, all these contradictions don't mean the Danes don't believe in environmentalism. They do. But it's common to many religions that the loudest professed believers often do the exact opposite in their personal lives.

Still, no one likes to talk about their own hypocrisy. So, at your next dinner Danish party, as you enjoy a tasty pork roast and discuss your host's fabulous recent trip to Thailand and compliment her new leather jacket, remember to work into the conversation how much you care about the environment. It's the right thing to do.

HOW I FINALLY LEARNED DANISH

AT FIRST, I COULD ONLY UNDERSTAND THE PUPPETS

I speak Danish. I have lived in Denmark for more than a decade, and I speak it reasonably well, or at least well enough to appear in my daughter's school play in a Danish-speaking role. Other foreigners frequently ask me for my advice on how to learn Danish.

It wasn't easy. For the first few years, I made plenty of mistakes.

THROWN OUT THE WINDOW

Like, for example, the time when I was forced to quickly leave a sublet apartment, and told everybody that I was not thrown out (*smidt ud*) but thrown out the window (*kastet ud*). Or like the time I went past the *Fødevareministeriet* (Agricultural Ministry) and, getting *fødevarer* confused with *fodtøj*, wondered why Denmark had such a big ministry for shoes.

That was before I coughed up for a private teacher, which was much better than the government-funded Danish-language schools I went through. Their programs were clearly designed for a 1963 type of immigrant: one made us repeat over and over, supposedly as a pronunciation drill, "*Jeg arbej-*

der på en fabrik i Vanløse." ("I work in a factory on the outskirts of town.") They also insisted on lumping candidates from all countries in a single class, being politically unwilling to accept that someone from Sweden might learn Danish a little faster than someone from Korea. As each day's class entered its third hour, the Swedish girl was drawing pictures in her notebook, while the guy from Korea was lost and gradually losing the will to live.

So, a private teacher, a student who cost about DK200 an hour, was best for me. Written Danish isn't too hard; it's straightforward and free of all the kaleidoscopic verb endings of Spanish and French, and the silly old-fashioned spellings of English.

ONLY A PART OF EACH WORD

Unfortunately, written Danish has absolutely nothing to do with spoken Danish. Danes, in a salute to Scandinavian minimalism, say only part of each word. Thus, what looks in your workbook like "*Hvad hedder du*?" ("What is your name?") is actually pronounced "Hv' hed' du?" Learning to understand spoken Danish is learning to guess which part of the spoken word is missing.

While you're trying to learn to understand spoken Danish, the best people to listen to are other foreigners. Other foreigners, in their ignorance, say entire Danish words. One of the first Danish speakers I could understand was Prince Henrik, who is originally from France. Danes hate the way he speaks Danish, but that's because he says the entire word, every time. I can also recommend watching hand puppets on television – since they have no real mouths, whomever is speaking for them needs to enunciate very well. Anything on TV in Danish with Danish-language subtitles for the deaf is also good. If all Danes came equipped with subtitles, life would be much easier for foreigners.

HVER DAG OG HVERDAG

Anyway, you might as well take mumbling as an advantage and mumble yourself. It makes it a lot harder for people to tell if you are making mistakes. I find it a particularly effective way of hiding my problems with adjective endings, i.e., the correct "*hver dag*" or the incorrect "*hvere dag.*" (By the way, "*hverdage*" (week days) does not really mean "*hver dag*" (every day of the week), as I found out when I tried to go to a "*Åben hverdage*" shop on a Sunday.)

At any rate, you will often be surprised to find Danes themselves differing about word use, comma placement, and other points of language: Danish may be formalized in books, but in daily use it is less so, perhaps because until recently no one has had the bother of teaching it to many foreigners.

Small disputes aside, the Danish language generally reflects the homogeny and harmony of Danish culture. That means no one ever says anything too definitively, for fear of having an unpopular opinion and being forced to back down.

I CAN SUFFER IT

For example, if something is good, you would say in English that you definitely and positively 'like it', but in Danish, you will say that you *kan lide* it, directly translated as you can suffer it. This construction keeps Danes from being unfashionably enthusiastic about things, and thereby assuming their opinion is more valuable than others, as proscribed by the Jantelov.

Also keep in mind non-committal phrases like *kunne godt være* (could well be), *i mine øjne* (in my eyes), and the all-time favorite, *blandt andre* (among other things). *Blandt andre* should be added to the end of every list to make sure no one will ever be able to accuse you of leaving something off the list.

WATCH OUT FOR O AND Ø

A few final tips. Watch the "o" and "ø" – for example, the *Mønster Bageri* near my home is trying to tell people that it is an excellent bakery (*mønster*), not that it is full of monsters.

Be careful about words that sound similar: after hearing a safety announcement on the 2A bus, I once tried to explain to a deaf old lady that "*en tyver*" (a twenty-cent piece) was in town picking pockets, when I should have said "*en tyv*" (a thief) was at fault.

And take special care when you use "*dufte*" (smell good) and "*lugte*" (smell bad) It's the same word – "smell" – in English, but people get real mad if you tell you can "*lugte*" the dinner they spent all day preparing.

Actually, there is a secret to learning Danish quickly, but it would horrify every Dane. That said, it assisted me enormously with grammar, vocabulary, and comprehension. I might never have learned Danish without it. The terrible secret is: learn German first. If you can speak English and German, functional Danish is only a few months of practice away.

HOLIDAY DRINKING STARTS NOW

THE TWO MONTHS OF CHRISTMAS

The Twelve Days of Christmas is an old French Christmas song. But those twelve days have nothing on the Danes, who have more than two months of Christmas, and would probably have it last all the way to spring if they could get away with it.

If you're in Denmark, you'll probably see the Christmas wrapping paper hit the shelves in mid-October, along with the first of the gingerbread Christmas cookies. A lot of Danish shops put out little dishes of brown Christmas cookies that look like overgrown M&Ms. Pepper nuts, they're called.

You're invited to take one – they're free, and they are very tasty. That said, you might not want to think about all the other little fingers that have touched those cookies. I recommend buying your own pepper nuts and enjoying them at home.

The official start to the Christmas season is in late October or early November, when Tuborg rolls out its annual Christmas beer.

It's released at precisely 20:59 on a Friday evening, and everybody between the age of fifteen and fifty hangs out in bars waiting for it, some dressed in blue Christmas beer hats, Christmas beer neckties, or even Christmas beer bikinis.

Christmas beer tastes a lot like regular beer, but a little bit sweeter, and a lot stronger. This is why a man I once knew, who was a bit of a wolf, told me that Christmas beer day was the best day of the year to 'score' with married women. The beer is very strong, and the ladies are guaranteed not to request that you call them in the morning.

I used to work at Carlsberg, which owns Tuborg, and I can tell you that the company had highly conflicted feelings about J-dag, which is what Christmas beer day is called. On one hand, it makes a mockery of their official corporate position promoting responsible drinking in moderate amounts. On the other hand, they do sell an incredible amount of beer on that day.

HEARTBREAK, FIGHTS, AND DANGEROUS ADVENTURES

So, if you're a party person, J-day is not to be missed. If you're a more quiet person, J-day is a good day to be home with the curtains drawn, wearing earplugs. If you're a Danish policeman, you'll be on duty that evening, sorting out all the heartbreak, fights, and dangerous adventures caused by Christmas beer. If you're a Danish taxi driver, you'll be cleaning up your cab several times.

And that's the start of Christmas season in Denmark. There will be lots of parties and lots of drinking, all the way through to January.

If you're new to Denmark, here's a tip: don't invite your friends to get together during the Christmas season. Don't plan a Christmas party, at least not one that includes Danes. Your friends are fully booked, particularly in December, with Christmas work events and Christmas family events and Christmas club events that were planned in August.

Throw a party in January, when everybody's miserable and broke. Then everyone you know will show up, even if all you serve is takeout pizza and leftover Christmas beer.

DANES AND BEAUTY

I get a little local newspaper in my mailbox every week, and this week – in between the usual stories about which local project has been able to squeeze the biggest subsidy out of the Copenhagen city government – there was an article about the Miss Denmark pageant.

Two teenagers from the neighborhood, one an ethnic Dane and one of Middle Eastern descent, had been selected to represent us in the pageant.

Now that surprised me. I've lived here for 17 years, and I'd never even heard of the Miss Denmark pageant. Denmark is usually not the sort of place where women in bathing suits walk around while fully-dressed men debate their merits.

And quite frankly, most Danes are less interested in the beauty of people than the beauty of *things*.

THE ARCHITECT-DRAWN HOUSE

If you really want to get a Dane all hot and bothered, start talking about some *thing* that is beautifully designed.

I do translations sometimes, from Danish to English, and recently I had to figure out how to translate the expression "arkitekttegnet hus" – literally, architect-drawn house.

Of course, all houses bigger than a mud hut are designed by some sort of architect, but that's not what the expression means.

An architect-designed house is something that's been designed specifically by the architect to match the owner's own vision. Often, it has modern, flowing lines, an open arrangement of rooms, and great big windows to let in light during the long Danish winter – and, inadvertently, let thieves see all the designer furniture inside.

A house like that celebrates the hand of the designer, makes the designer visible, and makes you look at the design and comment on it. That, to a Dane, is beauty.

THE BEAUTY OF THE PRACTICAL

In Denmark, beauty is usually found in something practical that has been very well designed. Housewares, particularly kitchenware, are a Danish design favorite.

They don't have to be from expensive materials, but they have to be simple, streamlined, and work flawlessly. The beauty is in the usefulness.

Danes also love unfussy furniture, durable fabrics with bright patterns, and soft rugs that are easy to clean.

A little high-design personal touch in a home is required too. I've seen bright copper coat hangers, crystal candle holders, and wooden monkeys. The nirvana is goods of extremely high quality, with maybe a slight twist of humor.

Interestingly, the Danes' passion for world-class home decor does not always extend to what's hanging on the wall.

It's quite common to see a Danish interior with some of the world's finest and most expensive housewares set off by amateur paintings done by the lady who lives there, or her adult daughter, or somebody's deceased great aunt.

Beauty as expressed in the fine arts, like classical painting and sculpture, is less of a passion in Denmark.

THE PLACE TO TAKE YOUR SECRET LOVER

The Vikings were not really oil painters, so the first real Danish oils were from about 200 years ago. They mostly depict young farmers and their love lives, and you can still check them out at the kind of museum that's popular with the over-70 crowd.

Modern art is much more popular in Denmark, particularly the contemporary interactive museums. Aarhus has a great rooftop rainbow you can walk through and see the city below in all different colors. Lots of families with kids there.

Less popular are museums of classical sculpture, like the Thorvaldsen Museum in downtown Copenhagen. Thorvaldsen was a Dane who went to Rome to learn to sculpt like an Italian, so the Thorvaldsen Museum is filled white marble shaped like strong-muscled warriors and soft-breasted naked nymphs in the Greek and Roman style.

Here's a tip: if you ever want to have an affair in Denmark, meet your sweetheart at the Thorvaldsen Museum. You and your secret lover will have the place to yourself. You might meet a couple Italian or Spanish tourists, but you won't meet anyone from Denmark.

Classical art celebrating the beauty of bodily perfection is just not very Danish.

DON'T EXPECT COMPLIMENTS

Now, Danes are OK with nudity, as long as it's ordinary, lumpy human nudity. But the idea of any human being an ideal doesn't fit well with their passion for equality, which suggests that no one person should be better than anyone else.

It's why you will rarely receive compliments of any sort in Denmark, and particularly not compliments on your looks.

Partly, that's because Danish men are very timid about possibly making a woman uncomfortable by praising her, uh, *structure.*

Partly because the Danish language does a poor job of describing beauty. Words like *flot, smuk, pæn, køn, yndig, fin,* and *lækker* don't have a lot of romantic flow to them.

And it's partly because physical beauty is something you're given, instead of having worked for, which makes it less valuable in Danish eyes.

But there's also a little bit of the Jantelov there, a little "how dare you be better looking than me?" To compliment someone's appearance might be to puff her up too much, make her think she's better than the others.

A few years ago, I wore a new and very expensive dress to a party, and while I had a good time, I was kind of miffed that no one mentioned my outfit. I said this to a Danish friend a couple of days later, and she confirmed that yes, she had noticed the dress, which she thought was beautifully made. "*But nobody said anything about it at the party*," I said.

"Why would we do that?" she said. "You already *knew* you looked good."

DANISH CHRISTMAS PART 2

THE CULTURAL IMPORTANCE OF THE ADULT ELF HAT

I've been living in Denmark so long I sometimes lose perspective. I forget what it's like to not live in Denmark. Specifically, I forget that in most countries, adult men and women don't want to walk around in an elf hat, even if it is Christmastime.

In Denmark, the red and white elf hat is part of any Christmas activity where alcohol is served, and even a few where alcohol isn't served. Children occasionally wear the elf hats, which are called *nissehue* in Danish. At my daughter's school pageant, the girls will wear long white gowns and carry candles for the Santa Lucia procession, and the boys will wear elf hats.

But you're more likely to see an elf hat on an adult, quite possibly on your boss or your professor or somebody else you're supposed to respect.

Wearing an elf hat as a grown-up in Denmark is a way to show you've got a sense of humor about yourself, that you're up for a party, that you see the fun in Christmas.

Or, that you can see any fun in life at all after four weeks of nonstop grey skies and rain during Danish November.

Elf hats are out in force during Danish corporate Christmas parties. You'll see them on the dance floor, or quite possibly see two of them making out in the printer room.

Danish corporate Christmas parties get pretty wild, which is why movers say their big season is December and January. One-half of a couple misbehaves at the Christmas party, and the movers are there the next weekend.

FRENCH PEOPLE DON'T WANT TO WEAR THE ELF HAT

Anyway, elf hats got me in trouble one year when I was trying to make a corporate video at Carlsberg, showing how our Danish division worked together with our French division to make a special Christmas beer.

The Danish team, including the executives, all wanted to be festive and wear elf hats. So, I asked the French team if they would, too.

Hmmm. Let's just say the French people did not want to wear the elf hats. I don't think I've ever seen angrier French people in my life.

But anyway, elf hats are not the only signs that Danish Christmas is on the way. There are braided hearts. Braided hearts are the little red-and-white paper ornaments that look like tic-tac-toe patterns. You're supposed to braid them together with your friends, at braiding heart afternoons, and then use them to decorate your home or your tree.

Another sign is the Christmas Calendar on Danish TV. The Christmas Calendar is a heartwarming show with a new episode every day during the Christmas season, which your Danish colleagues of all ages will watch and thoroughly discuss.

I have never watched one, and this disturbs the Danes around me because it's supposed to be a communal experience. One of the other mothers at school questioned whether or not my daughter was being properly raised if she couldn't watch the Christmas Calendar on TV.

BRING ALL YOUR MONEY TO THE DANISH POST OFFICE

One more Christmas experience you may be having is a little letter from the Danish post office, telling you that friends and family from abroad have sent you a Christmas present.

The little letter will say that if the present is worth more than 80 kroner, you need to pay 25% Danish value-added taxes on it, plus a 160 kroner administrative fee.

You could have avoided this by having your family buy online from somewhere in the E.U., like Amazon.co.uk, but now it's too late. Unless you want Grandma's homemade cookies and hand-knit sweater to be returned to her marked 'rejected,' you're going to have to go pick up the package and pay.

Depending on the shipping company she used, you may learn that the package can conveniently be picked up at inconvenient hours at a warehouse on the outskirts of town.

You and your money will follow the signs down a dusty concrete staircase to some odd office in the basement to find a wizened old postal clerk . . . and there's a good chance he'll be wearing an elf hat.

ØRESTAD, ØRSTEDS, AND ØRESUND

WHY I STILL GET LOST IN DENMARK

This week, I found myself running from *Sølvtoret*, where I mistakenly got off the bus, to *Søtorvet*, where my business meeting was. *Sølvtoret* and *Søtorvet* were about fifteen minutes apart by foot, and it was ten minutes before I had to be there, so I was moving pretty quickly.

It made me think about all the times I still get confused about Danish place names. A lot of names sound very similar to foreigners, although I'm sure to Danes they're quite distinct. For example, the Copenhagen metro has a stop called *Ørestad*, and one in another direction called *Øresund*.

Ørestad, Øresund. If you don't speak Danish well, two letters' difference is enough to get you very, very lost.

As a matter of fact, I've met and helped a lot of lost tourists, because *Ørestad* is a bit of a tourist attraction, with several examples of exciting modern architecture there. Another tourist attraction is a lovely garden called *Ørsteds* Park. Yes, that's right, folks – the difference is *Ørestad* or *Ørsteds*. And don't get frustrated and jump in the *Øresund*, which is the large body of water between Denmark and Sweden. The bridge between the two countries is the *Øresund* Bridge. *Ørestad, Ørsteds, Øresund.* Got it now?

I still haven't gotten it, because I still get lost. I missed a party recently because I went to *Nørregade* when I was supposed to go to *Nørre Allé*. I could have also gone to *Nørreport* or *Nørrebro*, all of which are within walking distance of each other in Copenhagen.

It's not just place names, it's people's names as well. Denmark having once been a very Christian nation, there are people with the last names Christensen, Christiansen, and Christianson. All of these people will be miffed if you get their name wrong.

First names can also be tricky. I got in trouble this week for calling a lady named Jytte '*Jette*' by mistake. She corrected me sharply. I still mess up the first names *Lene* and *Line*, and *Tina* and *Tine*. When it comes to men, it's easy to confuse *Jørgen* and *Jørn*, or *Mikeal* and *Mikkel*. And I do confuse them. All the time.

I even have problems with my own name in Danish. My name, Kay, which I pronounce to rhyme with 'day,' is spelled the same as a Danish man's name, *Kay*, which rhymes with 'pie.' Kay-rhymes-with-pie was a big name during the 1920s, so now it's associated with very old men, sort of like, say, *Elmer* in English. There are no young Elmers. Anyway, when I first got here, I tried to make an email appointment with a gynecologist, and was told, "Sorry, *Kay*! This doctor is only for women."

When Danish people do realize I'm a woman, they often call me not Kay, but *Kate*. I was helping some other parents paint my daughter's school recently, when I noticed that one of the fathers who was ordering all the mothers around kept calling me *Kate*. I corrected him – he's known me for years – and he immediately apologized.

"Sorry," he said. "There's an English lady named Kate where I work. All those English names sound alike. "

DANISH VIKINGS

OR, HOW TO FIND VIKINGS IN TODAY'S DENMARK

I play a little game sometimes when I look at Danish people. I imagine them as Danish Vikings.

It's easy now that big beards are in fashion on young men. Sometimes, on the metro, I'll look up at the hipster guy playing with his iPhone next to me and imagine him wearing a big fur cloak. Maybe with a rope belt and a sword dangling from it.

I imagine him stepping off the boat in Newfoundland in the year 1000, freaking out the local American Indians.

Imagining Danish women as Vikings is a little harder. They don't usually have the long braids or wear the big golden brooches that Viking ladies used to fasten their dresses. They don't wear the headscarves that married Viking women used to wear. Of course, you can still see plenty of headscarves in Denmark, but usually not on the Danes.

Anyway, the Danes love the Vikings, the same way the French love the age of the Impressionists or the British love the Second World War. It was a time when their country was at the peak of power and influence.

If you go to Denmark's National Museum in Copenhagen, you can spend hours looking at Viking handicrafts: lots of golden horns and rune stones. Danish kids learn a lot about the Vikings at school – even in kindergarten, they make Viking shields and swords, and try out Viking handicrafts.

There are various places around the country where you can 'live like a Viking' for a week. That means Viking-era food, Viking-era clothing, and Viking-era plumbing.

Unsaid in all this is that Vikings were not just fun guys who wore horned hats to soccer games. (Actually, they never wore horned hats at all; those hats were created in the 1800s by a man making costumes for Wagnerian operas.) The real Norse pagans were a gruesome people, by modern standards. Their religion involved a lot of human sacrifice, including young children, particularly young girls.

Viking, in fact, is the Norse word for 'pirate'. When these pirates took off on a raid in England or France, they stole everything they could, they burned down people's homes, and they hacked off people's limbs with axes. All that scary stuff you see in horror movies with fake blood, the Vikings actually did. These guys were not cute and cuddly. They were villains. They were bad guys.

Of course, your Danish friends will tell you, the people you'll meet in Denmark today are *not* the descendants of the Vikings. The Vikings, they'll tell you, were the guys who left. They settled in what is now England or France. The people you meet today in Denmark are the descendants of the people who didn't want to go anywhere.

DANES AND WORK

MY VACATION FLIGHT WAS CANCELLED
BECAUSE THE PILOT WAS ON VACATION

Going to church on Christmas Eve with the family is a hallowed tradition for Danes. For many of them, it's the only day of the year they go to church.

This past December, I arrived with a family friend to find the church was packed. Really, there weren't enough seats. People were forcing their way in, fighting for the best spots in a most un-Christian manner. An old lady with a cane was nearly pushed to the ground. We ended up with a seat near the back.

My family friend knew one of the ladies on the church vestry, who came by to say hello. And I, being a foreigner, said something along the lines of, "This service is so popular! You should probably add some more services on Christmas Eve next year."

The lady from the church smiled and shook her head. "That wouldn't be fair to the priests," she said. "The priests also need to spend time with their families at Christmas."

Now, I support priests spending time with their families. Priests need love too. But couldn't they spend time with their families on the 364 days a year when Danish people don't go to church and slip in a couple of extra services on Christmas Eve?

It's kind of their Super Bowl, their World Cup. It's their big day!

But this is part of a wider culture in Denmark, that the needs of the employee are often more important than the needs of the customer. This is great when you're an employee (reasonable working hours, extensive vacations) and exasperating when you're a customer. For example, most pharmacies are open from 9:30-5:30 on weekdays, and Saturday mornings only. Don't run out of meds on a Sunday!

This culture is changing, slowly. When I first came to Denmark, for example, all the shop clerks would take a lunch break at exactly noon – which, for course, was when all the customers who were on their lunch breaks wanted to buy things. You'd go to the stores and there would be no clerks. They were all off in the break room, eating their open-faced sandwiches from their *madpakker*.

That's less true now. Stores have learned to stagger their employees' lunch periods, although you'll still find most shops lightly staffed. Employees are expensive in Denmark, and Danish shoppers prefer to inspect the goods on display at their own pace without having a clerk pester them about buying something. If you can't get a shop clerk to pay attention to you in Denmark, don't take it personally: the Danes prefer passive sales personnel.

ARE YOU TAKING THREE OR FOUR?

When they're on the job themselves, Danes demand a lot from their workplaces. A full-time employee gets more than five paid weeks of vacation a year, six if you count the Danish public holidays; at least three of those weeks need to be taken during the summer, so you'll hear a lot of chatter in June about whether your co-workers will be taking 'three or four?' weeks this year.

Vacations are sacred time: they are never cancelled, and even top managers shut down their laptops for the duration. Employers also contribute to a vacation fund, so employees have a little extra cash to spend during their time off.

Companies also provide their workers with a private pension scheme and life insurance, and big companies will even pay for private health care so you don't have to wait in line for the public health service. Many employers also offer a lunch plan, so you can get tasty food at a low cost without leaving the office, and a fruit plan, so every employee gets a couple of healthy snacks per day.

These are seen as rights, not benefits. There was a front-page piece in the newspaper *Politiken* a while back about temporary employees who had not been given the enjoy-your-vacation payments and not been allowed to be part of the fruit plan. This was seen as really outrageous.

Danes are excellent workers. In fact, they're some of the most efficient workers in the world. They work very short hours, but they work hard. You rarely meet someone incompetent in Denmark.

But there's also a subset of people who act as if the job is there to serve them, instead of them serving the job. There was a famous case a few years ago: during the peak vacation season, July, the Scandinavian national airline SAS had to cancel a large number of flights. This was because too many SAS pilots had taken vacation - during the vacation season.

Now, SAS promised that would never happen again, and to my knowledge, it hasn't.

But, as I sat in my seat on an SAS plane last Christmas, waiting to be flown someplace sunny and warm, it was announced that the plane could not depart. There was a mechanical problem. And since it was the holiday season, all of the mechanics had the day off.

GOSSIP AND SCANDAL IN DENMARK

AND WHY DANISH POLITICIANS DON'T HAVE SEX SCANDALS

In general, Danes are not gossips, particularly about the sex lives of people they know. It's partly the Danish fetish for privacy, partly the basic acceptance of all things sexual, partly the lack of naughty excitement about all things sexual.

Danish politicians, for example, don't have sex scandals. French politicians have sex scandals. American politicians have sex scandals. Danish politicians have tax scandals.

They could be bedding down every night with a chimpanzee and the Danish media wouldn't touch it.

What the Danish public cares about is – *Are these guys paying every krone of their giant Danish taxes?* Because I am! They'd better be! Or did they or their spouse fail to meet the full non-residency requirement necessary to avoid the top tax on annual income? (That was a real scandal, by the way.)

THAT TIME I MADE A GOSSIP MISTAKE

Gossip is not really exchanged or enjoyed. A few years ago at an office party, I saw two co-workers who were married to other people leave the party with their arms around each other.

When I mentioned it to some other colleagues at lunch on Monday, their sudden silence made it clear that they felt the person who was behaving improperly ... was me.

There are some people whom, it is generally agreed, it's OK to gossip about. These are the people who appear in the weekly Danish color tabloids sold at every supermarket and kiosk. (One thing you should know about these magazines is that unlike supermarket tabloids in the USA, you're not allowed to flip through them while you wait in line. You touch them, you buy them.) These tabloids are also available for your reading pleasure at pizza joints and hairdressers all over Denmark.

This generally approved subset of gossip targets is relatively small. We're talking about anchors on the local news channels, football players and their lightly-clothed girlfriends, and the stars and judges of reality shows. In these weekly color tabloids, they openly discuss their romances, or lack of them, their children, or lack of them, their beach vacations, and the hats and dresses they wear to galas. There are a surprising number of galas in Denmark.

Nevertheless, it being a small country, you're bound to know some of these people personally sooner or later. I have an old friend who works for DR, the Danish public broadcaster, and while I was waiting in line at the supermarket to buy cat food, I found out that she was getting a divorce.

IT'S OK TO GOSSIP ABOUT THE ROYAL FAMILY

The real star of the weekly tabloids, and the foundation of all Danish gossip, is the Danish Royal Family. It's the world's longest-running soap opera – more than a thousand years on the throne and still going strong. In every weekly edition of the tabloids, you can count on several happy stories about the Royal Family. Happy, happy, happy. They are spending family time together! They are going to galas! They are an inspiration to us all!

Behind the happy family pictures, outside the tabloids, there is an undercurrent of royal gossip. Various princes are said to have different fathers than the officially announced candidate. Lots of examining family pictures there, comparing face shapes and eyebrows and noses and hairlines.

Another standard rumor is about the former Queen Ingrid, the current Queen's mother, who was supposedly a kleptomaniac. According to legend, she would go through stores and people's homes picking up items and putting them in her purse, and then a lady-in-waiting would come after her and pay for everything. None of this has ever been publicly confirmed, but everybody in Denmark knows the story.

And then there's nonstop chatter about the sex lives of the younger royals – whether they're happily married as they pretend to be or whether they're getting some on the side.

But if the Danish royal family wanted to take the focus off their potential sex scandals, there's one easy way to do it.

They could do something that royals in most other countries do, and, in fact, most people in Denmark do, and even some Danish politicians do.

They could pay taxes.

MORE SNOW TOMORROW

SURVIVING WINTER AS A FOREIGNER IN DENMARK

I'm looking out the window as I write, and it's snowing again. It's pretty, but it's not a novelty anymore. It's been like this for the past couple of weeks – Danish winter weather. Nearly every day, there's fresh snow and ice.

When I wake up on winter mornings, it's still pitch dark, very cold, and I can hear the wind whistling outside my window. Every day I think, "Ahhhh, I don't want to get up." But I do.

Of course, everyone in Denmark suffers a little bit during the winter. But I feel particularly bad for people who come from warmer climates and are experiencing one of their first winters here.

In Copenhagen the other day, I saw a pretty young woman – she looked like a newlywed – wearing traditional Pakistani dress. A light chiffon tunic, soft pajama pants, little leather slippers, and then a giant parka over the top. All around her was grey, slushy snow. I got the sense that she was a new bride whose husband hadn't really given her the full story about Denmark and Danish winter. She looked so cold and unhappy.

I also feel bad for the African migrant workers I see here. They're often wearing cool-looking leather jackets, which they probably get when they pass through Italy, and not much else in the way of winter clothing. I sometimes see one of these dark-skinned guys fighting his way through a white cloud of windy snow. And the look on his face is not full of love for Denmark.

Of course, immigrants to Denmark adapt to the cold after a while. I think Muslim women have it best, because they often wear a headscarf every day anyway.

Danes, on the other hand, often go bare-headed all winter. You see Danish people packed in like wooly Christmas presents, scarves, gloves, coats, waterproof boots, sometimes waterproof trousers, but no hat.

Amazing. And it's not just teenagers. I see elderly women in fancy mink coats (fur is acceptable in Denmark, by the way) and expensive leather gloves walking through the parking lot to their Audi or Mercedes – with no hat.

That said, there's still a lot to learn from the Danes on how to get through the cold winters.

First of all, if they can avoid them, they do.

Lots of people travel to warmer places during the winter, particularly the Danish Royal Family. When the weather is at its worst, they always seem to have an urgent ribbon to cut in the south of France, or Princess Mary's home country, Australia.

Ordinary people also do beach vacations, but ski vacations are big, too. You'll see people you know disappear for whole weeks in February to Switzerland or Norway. It's still cold in those places, but at least there's some sun reflecting off the snow.

MAKE A PLAN FOR THE DARK TIMES

For those of us who stay in Denmark, it helps to make a plan. It's good to choose a project for the 'dark times' – reading the backlist of your favorite author, learning a new software program, or watching an extensive playlist of comedy films on Netflix.

And February is a great time to invite friends over. Just like you, they have no plans and no money. Any day you invite them, they'll be there.

If you suffer from winter depression, which a lot of Danes do, you can buy a special white light that mimics the sun. I had one, and then I stored it away in the basement for summer and now I can't find it.

Instead, I occasionally go to tanning centers during the winter; not because I want to have orange, leathery skin, but because they deliver a little bit of that blue light I crave and haven't seen since September. I can really recommend it – it costs perhaps 40 kroner for 10 minutes – and I walk out of there feeling like I've taken a happy pill.

Anyway, you can learn to enjoy the winter in Denmark. There can be something comforting about a dark evening inside with a hot cup of tea or a glass of wine and a good book or movie.

And it's fun to watch kids in the snow. Kids of all ethnicities, pulling their sleds to the park to take a couple of trips down the hill. Kids making snowmen and throwing snowballs at each other. It's what kids do now in winter, and what they did a hundred years ago in winter, and probably what they will be doing a hundred years from now in winter. It's a classic.

DATING DANISH WOMEN

A GUIDE FOR THE FOREIGN MAN

I get a lot of mail from listeners of the *How to Live in Denmark* podcast, but a lot of it concerns one particular topic. Here's one from Teddy in Ghana: "I WANT TO KNOW IF DANE WOMEN WILL DATE A GHANAIAN MAN. I AM VERY MUCH INTERESTED." And one from last month, from Alex: "Hi, I'd like to know if Danish girls would date a Brazilian guy." And one from late last year: "I'm a gay African American male who would like to date a Dane. Any advice?"

Basically, a lot of the mail I get is from men wanting to know how they can get some action in Denmark.

I can understand this. Many Danes are beautiful. And I can tell you now, most of them will not immediately reject you because you have a different skin color. I know of several babies of mixed heritage here in Denmark.

While I can't offer any personal insights on gay dating in Denmark, I can tell you that male-female dating in Denmark is hard, even for the Danes, and it will probably be hard for you too.

That's because the romantic process that works in much of the rest of the Western world doesn't work in Denmark. In most parts of the West, a man will see a woman he likes and he'll approach her. He'll try to start a conversation. Maybe he'll ask if he can buy her a coffee, or a beer. If they're in a nightclub, he might ask her if she'd like to dance, or maybe go outside and get some fresh air.

These tactics will get you nowhere in Denmark. In fact, they will get you rejected, and then you'll worry that that you're being rejected because you're a foreigner. It's not because you're a foreigner. Danes are not good with strangers, any type of stranger. Generally, they don't talk to strangers. They talk to their friends.

I'll tell you how to get around this in a minute.

DON'T TELL HER HOW MUCH MONEY YOU MAKE

But first, let me tell you another thing that will get you rejected. I'll call it Manhattan or Moscow behavior, because it was the way men showed off for women when I lived in Manhattan, and my Russian friends say it's the way things work in Moscow today. Men tell a lady how much money they make, how much power and influence they have, and how much their car or watch cost.

This will get you nowhere in Denmark. First of all, if you have money in Denmark, the government's going to take it all away. The tax department will have your number, real fast.

Second of all, Denmark is a non-hierarchal society with a very flat structure. I think it's fair enough to say most women will prefer a man with a steady job, but saying you have a top management position just means that you have to spend a lot of time working and not as much time with your family and friends. That's not very Danish.

If you want to impress a Danish woman, talk about how your work benefits society at large, particularly how it benefits people who don't have a lot of resources.

For example, there are a lot of foreign engineers in Denmark. Don't tell a woman, as I have seen done, "Yeah, I'm an engineer. It's pretty boring." No, say, "*I'm an engineer, and I'm helping people in developing nations access clean water.*"

Another way to look good to a Danish woman is to show how your work benefits the environment. "*I'm a petroleum engineer. My job is to rethink drilling to minimize the danger to the environment.*"

Creative industries, like design, digital media, and video, are also seen as attractive in Denmark. Whatever you do, frame it in a way that shows how you're helping people. I really suggest that guys prepare a little speech to this extent before they start trying to meet women in Denmark. Two or three sentences, that's all it takes.

As a matter of fact, if you're hoping to meet women in Denmark, do a little preparation beforehand.

For example, check out how the local guys your age have their hair cut and what they're wearing. I've seen foreign guys in nightclubs with tight business shirts and shiny business shoes on, and they're getting nowhere. Do some reconnaissance first, maybe do some shopping. Danes are casual, but not sloppy.

And light on the cologne, guys. It's actually not necessary at all, but if you insist, use a very, very light touch.

Now, as I promised, back to how to meet women in the first place.

GET INTO THEIR CIRCLE OF FRIENDS

Danes aren't very good with strangers. They talk to their friends. What you need to do is come into their circle of friends.

Relationships are often born of the Danes' trademark long friendships. While a girl is unlikely to date the boy she has known since kindergarten, she might end up dating his brother, or the colleague that helped him move, or a guy who plays on his football team. So, if you're a man looking to date Danish women, make friends with a bunch of other guys, get invited to their parties and events, and then take it from there.

Once you're at a party, take advantage of the Danish tradition of shaking hands with every person in the room, saying your name with each new hand shaken, and then hanging out a bit with one of the guys you've just met. Talk to him about sports, the DJ, how he knows the host if you're at a house party.

After a few minutes of chatting with him, you can ask him about that great girl with the denim jacket whose hand you briefly shook, and if she's here with a partner. You know the lady's name, and now she's seen you with someone in her group, so you're not a complete stranger anymore.

Then go over and introduce yourself. Say you hear that she's a petroleum engineer whose job is to rethink drilling to minimize the danger to the environment. And that's fascinating because you really care about the environment. And I think you can take it from there.

This is somewhat how the Danes do it themselves, except that there's a lot of alcohol involved.

Basically, Danes go through all the same steps, but they're very shy, so they do it while drinking a bottle of wine or sometimes a bottle of vodka. If alcohol vanished from the Earth, so would romance in Denmark.

DATING DANISH MEN

A GUIDE FOR THE FOREIGN WOMAN

Before I tell you about dating in Denmark from the woman's perspective, I want to tell you a story about a movie I saw this week.

It was the latest in a long-running series called "Father of Four" *(Far til fire)*. The series has been running since the 1950s. As the kids grow up, they just replace them with new actors.

Anyway, in this particular episode of the series, there is a romance. The oldest sister, who's about twenty, meets a handsome young man with a guitar.

What struck me watching the movie was that the male romantic lead was visibly shorter than the female lead. I'd say at least three or four centimeters shorter, maybe more.

Now, in Hollywood, they'd have that guy standing on a box to look taller, or have the actress standing in a ditch to look shorter.

In the Danish film, there was no attempt to hide the height difference. They had the two lovers hold hands and walk side by side through a meadow, her head above his like a giraffe strolling across the savannah.

I had to admit, I couldn't focus on the love scene. I kept thinking, *"He's really short . . . or maybe she's really tall."*

In Hollywood, or Bollywood movies, the male actor is taller because he's supposed to be in charge, the dominant figure. But that's not true in Danish romance. The man is not in charge.

This means a lot if you're a foreign woman dating a Danish man. He is a not a Frenchman who will pursue you to the ends of the earth. He doesn't send flowers, he doesn't buy chocolates. He doesn't take you in his arms and kiss you until you're breathless. If you are a romance novelist, the Danish man is not your dream man.

On the other hand, if you're a 21st century feminist, a Danish man is your dream man. He will cook and help with the housework. He will take being a father seriously. He'll spend time with the kids. He'll take your opinion seriously. He won't force himself on you. In fact, you may have to force yourself on him. But if you do, he'll usually be really grateful.

CHIVALRY ISN'T APPRECIATED

Why are Danish men like this? I've asked my Danish male friends, and they say they're reacting to Danish women. Danish women, they say, like to do things for themselves. They don't want some clown opening the door for them or helping them carry packages. They can carry their own packages. My Danish male friends say that after offering to be chivalrous a couple of times and getting turned down in a nasty manner, they're reluctant to try anymore.

So, the Danish male approach is largely passive. They wait to see if the woman is interested. I get a lot of mail from non-Danish women trying to figure out if the Danish man they're dating is interested in them. "He's really happy when I call him, but he never calls me."

I honestly don't know what to tell them. I mean, I come from New York City, where men whistle at beautiful female strangers walking down the street. When I first moved to Denmark, I thought I'd stopped hearing whistles because I'd aged out of the whistle target group. But I've since established that beautiful young women in Denmark don't get whistled at either. Danish men do not want to offend women with their whistles.

NO THRILL OF THE CHASE

Now, I'm a modern woman, and I like a lot of things about these modern men. But they can occasionally err a bit on the soft side. Sometimes, Danish men seem too timid to do anything that makes men *men*, such as taking risks, taking initiative, or enjoying the pure thrill of the chase. Don't return a Frenchman's calls, and he will become intrigued and pursue you until the end of the Earth. Don't return a Dane's phone call (singular), and he will forget the whole thing.

A few weeks ago, we had a big storm in Denmark and it knocked down some large trees. Before the local government came to collect them, some people were sawing off bits for free firewood, or to make furniture, or for other arts and crafts projects.

On our street, a very large tree had fallen down, and as I was walking by that Saturday, I saw a young couple trying to take part of it home.

The small, slender young woman was sawing away at this big log with an old-fashioned manual saw while her muscular boyfriend just stood there, smiling, with his hands in his pockets.

Now, I don't know what was going on. Maybe he had a back injury – he was about twenty-five, so maybe he had a very youthful back injury. Maybe he was a professional hand model and couldn't risk damaging his fingernails on a messy metal saw. Or maybe he was a big wimp who was willing to let his girlfriend saw at a giant tree stump while he just stood there like a giant tree stump.

Given the general passivity of Danish men, it's hard to tell. I've done a lot of traveling, and I must say that the relations between the sexes in Denmark are the strangest I've ever seen.

FINDING A JOB IN DENMARK

SOME TIPS FROM MY EXPERIENCE

If you're a foreigner, finding a job in Denmark is not easy, but it can be done. It depends a lot on what you can do. And what you can do better than a Dane. Because, let's be frank here, if all things are equal between you and a Danish person, they're going to hire the Danish person.

The Danish person knows the language, the Danish person knows the culture, and the Danish person knows not to bring Brie cheese to the Friday shared breakfast. In every Danish office I've ever worked in, there's been a Friday shared breakfast, and they always eat exactly the same cheese. Sliced, medium-sharp Riberhus Danbo cheese.

Sometimes, I would try to bring a different cheese, and my Danish colleagues would smile and nod like they do when a foreigner has done something foolish . . . and then not eat my cheese.

They'd eat no cheese at all until someone brought out the medium-sharp Riberhus Danbo sliced cheese. My daughter and I call it "Danish-people cheese."

Anyway, the Danish workplace is about teams, working together, and getting along as a group, and there's an automatic suspicion that a foreigner might not fit into that dynamic. To overcome this, you have to show what you can do better than your Danish rivals.

If you have a diploma from a Danish university or trade school, that's a good start, because that's kind of a local seal of approval. If you're just moving here with a partner, you might want to consider this as a way to start out. Higher education is (in many cases) free here, and the government even gives you a stipend to live on while you learn. By the time you're finished with school, you'll have a network that should make job hunting easier.

Alternatively, I suggest you put all your effort into Danish classes at the start, and then get a job that will force you to speak Danish all day, every day.

I recommend working as an assistant in a Danish day care center. The jobs don't pay well, but they're relatively easy to get, particularly in Copenhagen, and particularly for men. They're always looking for men that the little boys can look up to. And quite frankly, the kids speak very simple Danish, and you speak very simple Danish. It's a good match.

JUST SPEAKING ENGLISH ISN'T ENOUGH

When people come from English-speaking countries – the U.S., Britain, Australia – they often ask me if just speaking English fluently is enough to get them a job. The answer is no, even though there are many companies that have English as their corporate language. But those are prestigious companies – Novo Nordisk, Lundbeck – places where everybody wants to work. You need to have excellent job skills, plus English, to work there.

So, if you do have a job skill plus English, and you want a job in Denmark, what do you do?

You can get an idea of what's out there by searching the job ads on databases like Jobindex.dk and WorkinDenmark.dk. But unless you're a perfect fit, don't rush to apply for these jobs. You'll be competing with dozens, possibly hundreds, of other people, many with spiffy Danish qualifications.

Instead, study the ads to figure out what skills companies are looking for. What skill can they not find? Figure out if you can dress up your CV to highlight some of those skills, or even take a quick course so you learn them.

Go to as many professional events as possible, chat with people, but don't ask them for a job. Ask them about your industry, ask them where the pain is in the industry, where the infuriating problems lie.

Then, write your job application letter (*ansøgning*) and your CV explaining how you and your skills can help them solve exactly the problem that everyone is worried about. Put the problems at the top and explain how you are the answer. Create a little elevator speech explaining how you and your skills can help solve this problem or that problem in your industry.

The local union that covers employees in your field can help with this, and can also help you adapt your CV and cover letter to Danish employers' tastes. Joining a union is well worth the money when you're looking for a job that requires an advanced degree.

And then start approaching companies, and be tough. The first time I was unemployed in Denmark, I approached 100 companies with personalized letters. I got about three responses . . . and one job, where I stayed for eight years. So, it's a numbers game.

DANISH PEOPLE LOVE LINKEDIN

Two more tips. Danish people love LinkedIn, so get your LinkedIn profile looking really spiffy. Please put up a professional picture. In just the small sample group of people who have asked for my help, I have experienced a variety of inappropriate LinkedIn profile images.

One guy had a picture of himself at a wedding, maybe his own wedding, wearing a white carnation. He looked like Fred Astaire. Another guy had a shadowy picture of himself at a nightclub, holding a beer.

Friends, you have to put up a clear picture of yourself smiling and looking pleasant and approachable in whatever type of clothing you wear for work. If you're a music producer, you don't have to wear a suit. If you're a banker, it's probably a good idea. Danes are casual, so a solid-color sweater or blouse is always fine, and so is *hijab* if it's simple and doesn't distract from your cheerful face.

Secondly, pay somebody to look over your LinkedIn profile and make sure it's in flawless English. I've hired people in Denmark, and it's always amazing to me that I get so many CVs and cover letters in terrible English, some of them from supposedly native English speakers.

So, that's my advice. It's hard to get a job in Denmark, but the good news is that everyone is rooting for you – particularly the Danish government. They want to get you working as quickly as possible so you can start paying your giant Danish taxes.

DANISH BIRTHDAYS

FLAGS, QUEENS, AND REMEMBERING TO BUY YOUR OWN CAKE

It has been said that Danish birthdays are the most important in the world. Adults, children, even the Queen of Denmark make a big deal about birthdays. And there is specific set of birthday rules and traditions for every age and role you play in life. Let's face it, Danish birthday traditions are a minefield for foreigners. Get it wrong and you could make some serious birthday faux pas.

For example, if the sun is shining on your birthday, you may find Danish people thanking you. "Thanks for the sunshine," they'll say. This is because in Danish tradition, the weather on your birthday reflects your behavior over the past year. If you've been good, the weather is good. If you've been bad . . . well, then. You get depressing, grey, Danish rain.

DANISH FLAG ON YOUR DESK

Even if it's raining, your Danish birthday starts first thing in the morning. Your family will wake you up with breakfast in bed and your birthday presents. Your good friends will send you text messages. You might even get a few birthday cards in the mail from older Danish ladies.

But you have responsibilities on your birthday as well. If you work in an office, you should bring cake or candy to share on your birthday. You can either bring this to an afternoon meeting or put out an email around 2pm saying that cake is available in the break room. Now, this was originally a little confusing for me, because where I come from, the colleagues buy the cake for the birthday boy or girl. In Denmark, you buy the cake. The same principle applies if you meet your friends for drinks after work – you buy the drinks to celebrate your birthday, not the other way around.

One thing your colleagues will do is put a Danish flag on your desk. Most offices have a small desktop Danish flag hanging around just for this purpose. In general, the Danish flag is closely linked to birthday celebrations, or in fact any celebration in Denmark. Some foreigners who are newly arrived misunderstand this as patriotism or nationalism. No, no, no. In this context, the Danish flag just means a party.

So, if someone is giving a party, they may put up a little pathway of paper Danish flags to guide people there. If you're invited to a party and aren't quite sure where it is being held, look for lights, music, and Danish flags.

KIDS GET LAYER CAKE AND TREASURE HUNTS

Danish children's birthday parties are usually pretty modest, compared to the competitive birthday parties you see in other countries, with magicians and bouncy castles and so forth. In Denmark, the kids eat some buns, play some games, eat some layer cake, go on a treasure hunt, and go home with a bag of candy. In my daughter's class, they actually do communal birthday parties – all the kids born in winter get together for one party, all the kids born in spring get together, etc. This is great, because everybody gets invited, and you have four or five other parents to help plan the party with.

Adult parties can also be very casual – depending on what birthday it is. If your friend is turning 18 or 27, there will probably be a lot of music or alcohol. All you need to do is show up in jeans and a T-shirt with some beer. If your friend is turning 38 or 47, there will probably be a Sunday lunch with a lot of family, and if you're invited too, all you need to do is show up in jeans and a sweater with some flowers or some cake or your kids. You don't really need to buy a gift, and if you want to, something small is fine – a book, or some fancy candy. One hundred or two hundred kroner is enough to spend for an ordinary Danish birthday.

BEWARE THE ROUND BIRTHDAY PARTY

But if your friend is turning 30 or 40 or 50, that's a whole different ballgame. That's a round birthday. It's a big deal. Your friend will throw a big party, hire out a room in a restaurant or even the entire restaurant, or put up a tent in the backyard and invite everyone she knows. Sometimes, in smaller towns, people will even put an ad in the newspaper, saying that anyone who knows the person having a birthday can just drop by for an open house. This can be fun: sometimes, people they haven't seen for 20 or 30 years turn up and say hi.

At any rate, for these round birthdays, the dress code is much more formal. Business wear for men and dresses or very fancy blouses for women, and much more expensive presents. I'd suggest a minimum of 500 kroner for a present for a round birthday. Buy your friend an elaborate photo book or DVD box set, jewelry, or a certificate for dinner in a fancy restaurant. (And get a "gift receipt" so the person can exchange it for something else; this is considered OK in Denmark.) Keep in mind, if you get a formal invitation to a round birthday, it's a sign that the person holding a birthday sees you as a close friend, so you should definitely show up if you can.

Of course, some people don't want to hold a party, for various reasons. And if they don't, it's become a trend to plan a trip abroad to celebrate the round birthday. I know one family with a parent turning 40 who went to New York, and another one with a parent turning 60 who planned a sunny charter vacation to Turkey. Getting away on a round birthday is actually what I do. I'm not much of a party giver, so on my last round birthday, I took a chocolate-shopping trip to Brussels.

Anyway, if you don't go away on your round birthday and make a big deal of it, people will think it's odd that you're not inviting them to a party. Or they may wonder if there was a party you didn't invite them to.

PEPPER AND CINNAMON

Now, that's the basics of Danish birthdays. But there's the advanced class, too: for example, if a Dane isn't married by age 25, his friends douse him or her with cinnamon on his 25th birthday. (You'll find Danish-language guides on the internet for how to get large amounts of cinnamon out of your clothes.) At age 30, it's pepper. You get doused with pepper on your 30th birthday if you're not married. And there are regional variations, too – on the island of Fyn, there's a special type of brown cake, *brunsviger*, that's served on every birthday.

But the most important advanced birthday etiquette surrounds the Queen. At noon on April 16 of each year, she and all the members of the royal family in good standing (or the ones she likes) go out on the balcony at one of her castles and wave to the crowds below.

You can join the crowd too – your only job is to wave back. And remember to bring your best birthday accessory: a bright red Danish flag.

DANES AND SPRING

HOT WHEAT BUNS AND HIGHLY-EDUCATED DRUNKS

It's spring in Denmark, and spring is by far my favorite season here. The wonderful white Scandinavian sunlight is back after the dark days of the winter, the flowers are coming out on the trees, and everybody's in a good mood. The outdoor cafés are full of people again – sometimes draped in blankets to keep warm, but outside all the same.

April and May are often the best months for weather in Denmark, along with September. Summers can be rainy. And April is when Tivoli opens in Copenhagen. (Side note: when you see a man in Denmark with his trousers accidentally un-zipped, you quietly inform him, "Tivoli is open!")

Tivoli is one of the world's great non-disappointing tour-ist attractions – it's constantly updated with new shops, new rides, fresh flowers, and fresh restaurants. And in the spring, it's not as crowded as it is in the summer. You can hang out all day, have a picnic, ride the rollercoaster, and even hear some bands play.

And you'll have time to do that, because spring is when the Danes' public holidays really stack up. There are three public holidays around Easter – Thursday, Friday, and the following

Monday – and then several other public holidays, like Ascension Day, and the Friday after it. And Whitsunday, and the Monday after it.

DANISH FUNDAMENTALISTS LOVE BIG PRAYER DAY

Plus Big Prayer Day, which is in late April or early May. Big Prayer Day is a Danish-only holiday, and there have even been suggestions that it should be eliminated in order to save money for the government, or even introduce a new Muslim holiday to go along with all the Christian ones.

Technically, there's no reason that Muslims or Buddhists or Jews couldn't all pray along on Big Prayer Day, but Big Prayer Day's origins are Christian. The day was a compromise. In the olden days, all sorts of guilds were laying down their tools for their own prayer days at inconvenient times, so it was decided to roll all the individual prayer days into one Big Prayer Day.

Big Prayer Day has its own traditions. For example, you're supposed to take a walk on Big Prayer Day. At one point, it was a walk around the Copenhagen city ramparts, but now it's just a walk, anywhere. And Big Prayer Day has a special food, known as Hot Wheat Buns. Originally, bakers were closed on Big Prayer Day, so you would get your Wheat Buns the night before and heat them up on the day. Traditions like this are now mostly observed by Danish fundamentalists.

Anyway, when I first came to Denmark, I arrived right before all of these big holidays, and I didn't know anyone and I was living in a hotel and I thought – what do people do with all these holidays? Now I know. You take a walk, or a bike trip. You go to Tivoli. You go to your Danish summer house. Or, if you're 14 years old, you get confirmed.

CONFIRMATION: RELIGIOUS EVENT OR CONSUMER EVENT?

Spring is also confirmation season in Denmark. In the Christian religion, confirmation is when you take responsibility as an adult within the church. So, thousands of Danish teenagers, having spent the winter learning the names of Old Testament prophets and Jesus' disciples, are ready for confirmation in the spring.

On each Sunday or public holiday in April or May, Danish churches are filled with up to 40 kids at a time going through confirmation ceremonies – the boys in new suits, the girls in pretty dresses. Now, as I've noted, Danes are not particularly religious. You might ask – what's with the big church service?

The deal is, each confirmation is followed by a party, a big party. Every member of the teenager's extended family is invited, and all of them are expected to bring money. Gifts of money are part of the confirmation experience, probably the best part if you ask the teenagers.

Then the day after the ceremony, the kids are allowed to skip school and go shopping to spend all their new cash. This is called 'Blue Monday,' and it's an accepted indulgence and a great driver of the Danish economy. Shopping malls order extra clothes and electronics for the wave of teenage shoppers. I've even seen some local tourist boards offer Blue Monday package trips for confirmation kids from the countryside.

Of course, the confirmation service also has some advantages for the Danish church: it gets potential worshippers through the door right before they're 18, which is when they often decide whether or not to pay church tax. Church tax is one of the few optional taxes in Denmark, but if you don't pay it, you don't get access to church services. Danish priests often refuse to bless the burials of people who didn't contribute to the church coffers while they were alive.

HIGHLY EDUCATED DRUNKS

As spring fades into summer, another familiar sight appears in the streets of Denmark: slightly older teenagers wearing distinctive canvas white caps. These kids are now officially *students*, in the Danish phraseology, which means that they have just finished their secondary education.

The different colors of cap or ribbon on the cap indicate what type of education has been completed: bordeaux color for an academic secondary school, royal blue for business school, dark blue for technical school.

Each school of students rents a giant open-back truck and drives around town to every single classmates' home, singing, screaming, and honking horns. If you're taking a Saturday afternoon nap, a truck of students driving by will wake you up. The students have a drink at each stop, so by the end of the day, they're pretty much falling off the truck.

In my country, the United States, the liability lawyers would be all over this. One drunk kid would fall off the truck, sue the school, and the tradition would be ended forever.

But this is Denmark, and spring traditions live on.

THE LITTLE MERMAID IS A DISAPPOINTMENT

BETTER IDEAS FOR TOURISTS AND OTHER VISITORS

More than 9 million people visit Denmark ever year, and if you live here long enough, some of those visitors may be your relatives or hometown friends.

What do you do with them? Whether they come by cruise ship, car ferry, express train or budget airline, they all want the Danish experience.

Based on my many years of showing parents, aunts, former colleagues, old college roommates, and friends of friends around Denmark, these are my tips.

THE CLASSIC TOURIST DAY

First of all, start your tourists in the morning with a trip to the local bakery where they can pick out their own Danish pastry. Or two or three pastries. Even though they're called *wienerbrød* – 'Viennese bread' – in Danish, Denmark's pastries really are some of the best in the world, entirely unlike the plastic-bag versions of 'Danishes' you'll find in other countries. And get some coffee or black tea. Carbs and caffeine will set your tourists up well for the day's busy program.

Once your tourists are energized, now is the time to take them walking. Walk them around the old city center and past the largest, most visible historical monuments in your town. In Copenhagen, you can take them up the Round Tower or to Amalienborg Palace; in Aarhus, maybe tour the *Gamle By* or the rooftop rainbow at AROS museum. In Odense, anything related to Hans Christian Andersen is bound to be a hit.

Now, part of this trip may take them down a shopping street. This is critical – don't let them shop yet, or they'll be carrying bags around all day. Or, if it's your mom, you'll be carrying bags around all day. Save the shopping for another time.

TIME FOR LUNCH

After you've seen the city and the major sites, it might be time for an early lunch. If the weather is good, a picnic in the park is great. Denmark has beautiful parks. Maybe buy some Danish open-faced sandwiches and some drinks.

If your visitors are elderly – or if they're rich and will be picking up the tab – a touristy restaurant with Danish food is another option. Look for one with several different types of herring on the menu, which makes them feel authentic, plus some other food that your guests can actually order once they've confessed that they don't like herring. *Stjernskud* on the menu is always a good sign: it's a mild fried fish that's pretty enough to photograph and unambitious enough for most people to eat.

Your tourists are now re-energized, so now is a great time for the local museum. As a general rule, I find that young men and boys can be coaxed into museums with talk about Viking artifacts — lots of scary-looking armor and sticks with points on the end. Older or quieter tourists will probably like the Danish design museums. Copenhagen has the biggest one, with everything from chic mid-century furniture to posters to fashion, but even small towns often have an art or glass museum.

After an hour or two in the museum, it's probably late afternoon. Your tourists are getting a little tired. I recommend a boat trip. Your guests can sit down with a chilled Danish beer and see the city from the water. In Copenhagen, these boat trips are a great way to see Denmark's most disappointing tourist attraction, the statue of the Little Mermaid.

If you've seen it, you know the Little Mermaid is only about four feet tall – that's 1.25 meters. You probably own pillows that are bigger than the Little Mermaid. But all the boat trips go right by it, so your tourists can get the photos they need for their Instagram or Facebook feeds. If they want, they can climb out of the boat and onto the slippery rock where the mermaid sits for a photo. That's best performed before too many beers have been consumed.

You can round out the day at one of the local music festivals, or Tivoli if you're in Copenhagen. After that, you're on your own – I'm afraid I can't offer you any nightlife recommendations. Ask someone under thirty who doesn't have any kids.

DANES AND SINGING

DANISH DRINKING SONGS, PARTY SONGS, AND
FOREIGNERS WHO TRY TO HUM ALONG

There have been very few international singing stars from Denmark, and that's rather odd, because Danish people love to sing.

Joining choirs is very popular, and Danish schoolchildren often start the week with a song. In my daughter's school, all the grades get together and sing something from the school's common songbook.

There's actually a kind of common songbook for all the children of Denmark, called *De Små Synger* ('The Small Songs'), where you can find classics like *Se Min Kjole* (See My Dress), *Lille Peter Edderkop* (Little Peter Spider), or *Oles Nye Autobil* (Ole's New Car). Ole's new car is actually a toy car that he uses to run into things, like his sister's dollhouse.

In general, the Small Songs are a throwback to an older Denmark, a quieter Denmark, where most people lived in the countryside. Many of the songs refer to green hilltops, baby pigs and horses, or happy frogs that live in a swamp. And, of course, all the humans in the Small Songs are entirely Danish – or 'Pear Danish,' as the local expression goes. One out of five children born in Denmark today has a mother who is not an ethnic Dane, but there's no such thing as *Little Pavel Spider* or *Muhammed's New Toy Car*.

Still, everyone who grows up in Denmark learns these songs. And other songs that are just part of the Danish canon. Back when I was looking around for a school for my daughter, I went to a parent introduction meeting where the principal asked everyone to start by singing *The Autumn Song*. All the Danish parents got up. There were probably 200 of them there, all smiling, brought back to their school days. They happily sang the song. They all knew the words. I had no idea what was going on, so I just stood up and hummed along.

DANISH DRINKING SONGS

But Danish singing is not just for children. Danish teenagers and young adults, who tend to drink a lot, love Danish drinking songs. 'Snaps songs' are made to be sung right before drinking a shot of snaps, and they're an important part of Danish student culture. One you'll probably hear is *Sail up the river*. The lyrics are easy to learn: 'Sail up the river, sail down again. That was a great song, let's sing it again.' And then, of course, you sing it again. Many times. My neighbors were doing that last weekend.

Danish adults don't have to be drunk to sing. If someone has a 'round' birthday – 30, 40, 50, 60 – or is retiring from her job after many years, it's considered good manners in Denmark to write them a song. You don't have to write the melody, you just use one of those Danish songs that everyone knows. And then you write lyrics that gently satirize the person's lifestyle or interests, plus how much you care for them – if it's a birthday – or how much you'll miss them – if it's a retirement.

The good news is, you don't have to write these lyrics yourself. Some people do this professionally. You can Google '*festsange*' and you'll find dozens of people using Google Adwords to sell their services. It costs about 400 kroner to get a song written for your event, and the songwriter will ask you for a few light-hearted stories about the person being celebrated – like he's good at fixing things around the house, or she's very messy and can never find her car keys. It doesn't go much deeper than that.

SINGING SONGS ABOUT YOURSELF

So, when it's time for the party, there will be a copy of the song for everyone attending, and you'll all stand in a circle and sing it. I usually don't know the song they're singing along to, but I hum at the beginning and then just pick up the melody by the second or third verse, and there are usually around seven verses long. You get tired by the end. One thing I find funny is that the person being celebrated generally stands there with his own piece of paper singing along to the song about himself. And at the end, everyone raises their glasses for a toast. 'Skål!'

CAT BITES AND DENTAL VACATIONS

THE UPS AND DOWNS OF THE DANISH HEALTH CARE SYSTEM

I've just arrived back in Denmark after a couple of weeks in the U.S., and the night I got back, my cat bit me. This was not just a little affectionate peck – Fluffy used her sharp teeth, her fangs, to create four bleeding puncture wounds in my leg. I suppose it was partly my fault – I put a call on speakerphone. Fluffy doesn't like speakerphone, because she can hear a person but she can't see one, so she assumes I'm some evil magician who has put a person inside a little glowing box. And she bites me.

So I was bleeding, and I did what I did the last time she bit me – which was a couple of months ago, the last time I used speakerphone. I called 1813, the Danish government's non-emergency line for off-hour medical situations.

I waited about five minutes for a nurse to take the call, and she asked me some questions about the size and location of the bite, and whether or not I'd had a tetanus shot recently. I hadn't, so she made an appointment for me at the local emergency room for about an hour later.

ROBOT CHECK-IN

When I got to the emergency room, there was no human being to greet me – just a very tall robot with a scanner. I scanned my yellow Danish health card. The machine said 'beep' and automatically put me in line according to the seriousness of my injury. (Which was not all that serious.)

I waited a half hour or so. Then I was seen by Nurse Andrea, who examined the bite and then referred me to handsome Dr. Rasmus.

Handsome Dr. Rasmus was the highlight of the evening. He had a great bedside manner, and gave me a shot and enough penicillin to last the evening. Then he sent me home with a prescription so I could go to the pharmacy to pick up more penicillin, just in case Fluffy had some bacteria on her small teeth. And that was that, until I use speakerphone again.

HEALTH CARE QUIRKS

This type of situation is when the Danish health care system works well. There are no forms to fill out, no insurance to hassle with, and no payment of any kind. In general, the Danish system is excellent with things that have to be handled right away. They're quick and efficient. I've even heard of tourists who have, say, broken an ankle in Copenhagen and come back raving about the health care they received.

And, of course, it's all tax-funded. (I hate it when people say Danish health care is 'free.' I pay some very serious taxes for all this 'free' stuff.)

But the Danish health care system has some quirks. First of all, if something doesn't have to be handled right away, it isn't. There used to be long waiting lists for cancer treatment, which have mostly been eliminated, but if you're looking for knee surgery or a cataract operation or any other treatment that doesn't require instant action, it can take a while.

First, your own doctor has to send you to a specialist, and getting an appointment there can take three or six months, and then after that you'll have to wait for an appointment for surgery. (A convenient website lets you know the waiting time at various hospitals.) When you do get an appointment, the Danish health service picks the time and date, and you'd better be there. If you have other plans, they'll give your time to someone else on the list.

Another quirk is that the Danes are not really into active treatment of small illnesses. For colds and the flu, they like hot tea and hot rum, staying home from work, and not really anything else. So, if there's something special from your home country that you find comforting when you get sick, I recommend you bring it with you.

Doctors in Denmark are also very reluctant to prescribe any kind of antibiotic, sleep medication, or prescription painkiller. They generally just tell you to take ordinary ibuprofen or Panadol that you can get at the supermarket. I had a C-section when I gave birth to my daughter, and that's what I got – ibuprofen and Panadol.

You can ask your doctor for something stronger, but there's no guarantee you're going to get it, and if you do, you're going to have to pay for it yourself. (Don't ever order medicine through the mail from other countries; this is considered 'drug smuggling' and if the stuff is caught at customs you will get a Danish police record and a fine.)

Dentistry is not covered by the public health system, at least for adults, and it's so expensive in Denmark that it's very common for people to go to on a 'dental vacation' to Poland or Hungary. Probably not for an annual check-up, but if you need major dental work, it is sometimes actually cheaper for you and a friend to fly to Krakow or Budapest or even Prague and get your teeth done, and even work in a little sightseeing.

SUMMERHOUSE OR DOLL HOUSE?

WHAT TO EXPECT IF YOU'RE INVITED TO A DANISH SUMMER HOME

I f you live in a city or a big town in Denmark, you may notice that summer weekends are very quiet.

The streets outside my home in Copenhagen are empty. The traffic lights just change from red to green and back again, but no cars ever pull up. Nobody comes to cross the street. It's a little like a scene in a movie right after the zombie apocalypse.

This is because all the Danish people have gone to their summerhouses.

On Friday afternoons, Danish people like to pack up their cars, drive out to the countryside, and spend the weekend in conditions that are sometimes quite primitive.

Every summerhouse is different, but most of them seem to have questionable plumbing, odd sleeping arrangements, and chipped dishes and glassware.

The Danish summerhouse is an old tradition – four hundred years ago, the King started offering small plots of land to the people who lived in crowded, sooty cities. The idea was that they could get away to the clean, fresh air on weekends and grow healthy vegetables.

Fast forward to now, and very few people grow vegetables on their plots anymore. Instead, these small summerhouse plots have become little kingdoms with neatly clipped hedges all around and lots of lawn chairs and flowerbeds and bird feeders. In the center is a tiny, tiny house – usually not more than fifty square meters, or 400 square feet – where the entire family spends the summer.

This little doll house is almost always lovingly taken care of, with freshly painted, clean windows, flowery curtains. I've also seen elaborate summerhouses. One near my house has a copper roof, like a cathedral or a courthouse. When I was looking at real estate ads for this story, I saw another one that had been fitted with big white columns like the mansion house in *Gone With the Wind*.

DO MAXIMUM-SECURITY PRISONERS GET MORE SPACE?

But as fancy as summerhouses can be, they are small. There's usually room for one double bed or a fold-out couch, and then maybe there's a loft where a couple more people can sleep, maybe a porch for one or two more. I would guess that Danish maximum-security prisoners get more sleeping space than ordinary Danes in their summerhouses.

Before I go further, I should explain that there are actually two types of summerhouse. One type, sometimes called a *fritidshus*, or 'free-time house', is really in the countryside. It can take several hours to drive there from the family's main home.

The other kind is what's called a 'colony garden' – *kolonihave* – and these tend to be in, or close to, the major cities. If you take the S-train through the northern part of Copenhagen, for example, you'll see all sorts of little shacks down by the railroad tracks. (That sounds like a Dolly Parton song, doesn't it? ♫ *I got a little shack by the railroad track.* ♫)

But these shacks are not the homes of poor-but-cheerful banjo players. They are colony gardens, and the people who own them have at least one other home and money enough to take care of two.

LOTS OF JENSENS AND HANSENS, FEW EL-HASSANS

Each colony garden is part of an association run by volunteers, which maintains the waiting lists to get a plot. These waiting lists are hundreds of people long, and they read like the Danish phone book of 1957. Lots of Jensens and Hansens and Larsens and not many El-Hassans, although there are a few. Still, colony gardens are an ethnic Danish phenomenon. You'll notice a lot of the plots have very tall flagpoles with very large Danish flags.

If you don't want to wait for your colony garden, you can buy one. I saw one on sale this week for 700,000 kroner– that's about 94,000 Euro, or 100,000 U.S. dollars. The house is 45 square meters – 500 square feet – and it has no toilet. But the ad says you can install one if you want. Of course, you can only use the toilet from May to September. This is the big difference between colony gardens and other summerhouses – you are not allowed to live in a colony garden year round. They turn off the water in the winter to make sure.

One thing I, as a foreigner, have never understood is what you do in a colony garden or a summerhouse. Supposedly, it's about getting away from it all. I guess you can read, or sit in the sun, or play board games when it rains. You can always invite the family over for a big Sunday lunch.

But I have a theory about the real reason summer houses are so popular in Denmark. Danes like nothing more than to fix up their houses, and when they buy a summerhouse, they have two houses to fix up. You know, they can cut the grass, they can make more flowery curtains, and they can go out and buy chipped glassware at the local flea market.

Fixing up a summerhouse can keep a Danish person happily occupied all summer.

SALAAM AND GODDAG

MUSLIMS IN DENMARK

There's a new mosque opening down the street from me this spring, a big one. It will be the first mosque with minarets in Denmark, although the minarets are legally prohibited from calling to prayer.

The people behind the mosque are doing everything they can to blend in with the local neighborhood – they even went to observe at a local church service a couple of Sundays ago. They were probably the only ones there.

There are a lot of Muslims in Denmark, about 270,000 out of a population of million, most of whom have arrived here in the past 40 years.

And contrary to what the Danish right-wing parties might say, they've brought a lot of good things to Denmark, and not just Shwarma shops.

MILK ON A SUNDAY

Corner kiosks are largely a Muslim innovation in Denmark. When I first visited Denmark in 1984, all the shops closed at 5:30pm on weekdays and 2pm on Saturdays, and they were closed all day on Sunday. If you ran out of milk on a weekend, you had to borrow from a neighbor or just drink beer until Monday morning. The kiosks run by Muslim immigrants changed all that.

These days, Muslim women in particular have a lot to offer to Danish culture. If you go into any pharmacy in Denmark, you will probably find at least one female pharmacist wearing a headscarf.

I had a similar experience when I did a tour of the Rigshospitalitet, Denmark's largest and most prestigious hospital, where all the royal babies are born. In the bloodwork division, almost all the workers were Muslim women wearing headscarves.

This is a way for devout Muslim women to join the medical field without having to touch men or see men unclothed. I thought that was great.

As a matter of fact, the statistics show that girls from second generation and third generation immigrant backgrounds in Denmark now attain equal educational credentials to ethnic Danish girls. Not all those girls are Muslims, but a lot of them are.

HIJAB ON A BICYCLE

Sure, there are still problems and tensions mixing Danish cultures with Muslim traditional cultures. *Niqab* is always going to be an outlier in a culture where showing your face, shaking hands, and making direct eye contact is seen as a sign of honesty and dependability.

Even women wearing less strict modest clothing face challenges in Denmark. Depending on the clothes they choose, it can be difficult to ride a bicycle. Some Muslim women feel modest enough in long loose pants, and that works fine, but others feel a long skirt is required, and that works less well. Riding a bicycle is the key to freedom in Danish cities – it means you can get around cheaply and safely just about anywhere. If you don't, you're stuck waiting for the bus. Whenever I'm stuck waiting for the bus, I see a lot of women in long, dark skirts waiting with me.

Avoiding *haram* food will also take some effort. Pork is an important part of the Danish diet; it's even an ingredient in some baked goods. And alcohol is an important part of Danish socializing. While it's bad for business to avoid every event where alcohol is served, a lot of Muslims I know arrive early, bring their own non-alcoholic drinks or stick to soda, and leave before the party gets out of hand. (One tip is to spend your time chatting with the people who have to drive their cars home; they can't drink any alcohol either.)

CAN YOU LIVE THERE?

At *howtoliveindenmark.com*, I get a fair amount of email from Muslims who have written to me, asking if Denmark is a good place for them to live.

It is a good place. All the things that are good about Denmark for other people – that it's a peaceful country, a safe country, a country where you can earn a good living and still have time for your family – are also good for Muslims.

DANES MUST ADAPT, BUT MUSLIMS MUST ADAPT TOO

I also tell the people who write to me that, in a multicultural world, it's fair enough to ask the Danes to adapt to and accept different ways of living, but you have to adapt and accept, too.

People dress the way they want to in Denmark. The women usually wear less clothing than in Muslim-majority countries, particularly in the summer, and that does not indicate that they're available to any man who asks. That's just what they're comfortable in, just like women you know may be more comfortable with *hijab* or other traditional dress. You must accept this. There's nothing worse for intercultural relations than Muslim guys harassing Danish women for wearing Western clothing or even touching them without their permission – something I've unfortunately experienced myself.

Women in Denmark also date whomever they like, for short and long periods, and they never have to ask their parents or brothers for permission. They sometimes choose the wrong guy (something else I've unfortunately experienced myself), but if they do that they're free to just move along to the next guy. It's up to them.

I also tell the people who write to me that if you live in Denmark, you have to be able to accept gay people. Gay people here get married and they have children, and those children are going to play with your children. They're going to invite your children – and maybe you – to their homes. If that's not something you can handle, your children are going to be lonely. They're not going to fit in. And they're less likely to be successful in school.

MEN DO HOUSEWORK IN DENMARK

Finally, the roles of men and women are different than they are in Muslim countries. Most married women work outside the home in Denmark. The tax system is set up so it's very difficult for one income to support a family. And very few people have servants in Denmark. That means that even educated, well-off people do most of their own housework. Men, too. Educated, well-off men do cleaning and cooking and daily care of children. This is very unusual in most of Asia, the Middle East, and Africa. In Denmark, it's expected.

I read in the newspaper about a small Danish company that hired an Iranian engineer. At this particular company, everyone would eat breakfast together on Friday morning. After the breakfast was finished, they would take turns cleaning up the dishes and wiping off the table. Everyone took a turn, including the CEO himself. When it was the turn of the Iranian engineer to clean up, he quit. "*I'm an engineer,*" he said. "*I'm not a cleaning lady.*"

In Denmark, that's not true. In Denmark, everybody's a cleaning lady.

DANES AND NORWEGIANS

BITTER ENVY AND BROTHERLY LOVE

Although I've chosen to live in Denmark, I have a personal relationship with Norway. My grandmother's family comes from Norway, and as my mother was growing up, her mother told her that our family was Norwegian royalty.

Never mind that there was no modern Norwegian royalty until 1905, when the country became independent, and our family came to the U.S. thirty years before that. My mother grew up being told she was a lost Norwegian princess. I think it was something that her grandparents, who were immigrants, did to make their kids feel special.

Fast forward sixty years, and my mother and her sister, who would, of course, also have been a Norwegian princess, got a chance to visit Norway for the first time. My mother, who has a good sense of humor, wore a crown on the plane. She and her sister got crowns at a costume store and wore them on the SAS flight to Norway. She said the stewardesses really loved it. When they got off the plane, they did the royal wave. And they went to the Royal Palace and had their picture taken out front, wearing their crowns.

So, bottom line, I'm not sure the Mellish family is welcome in Norway anymore.

FAMILY ENVY

Danes and Norwegians were part of the same country for hundreds of years, and they're still family. Written Danish and written Norwegian are very similar – so similar that I once tried to find a Danish-Norwegian dictionary and was told there was no such thing. The spoken language is a little more different, but Danes and Norwegians can usually understand what the other is saying.

Danes and Norwegians like each other. They care about each other. They sometimes even cheer for each other's soccer teams.

But like any family, there's envy involved. Envy.

For example, there's envy of each other's geographical pleasures. Norway has beautiful mountains, great for skiing. Denmark has windswept beaches, which the Norwegians seem to love. Lots of summer holidays are spent in Denmark.

Denmark has Copenhagen – which, let's face it, is a cooler city than Oslo. It just is. Sorry, Oslo.

But Norway has those beautiful, isolated towns on the fjords, with their brightly-colored wooden houses and their long summer nights. If you know any Danish doctors, you'll know that they frequently take a week or two off and go work in one of those isolated Norwegian towns, where they make a lot of money.

And now we come again to the envy in the relationship. Norway has money. And it didn't used to have money.

For hundreds of years, Denmark was sort of the big brother in the Danish-Norwegian relationship.

Even the Norwegian royal family – the real one – is descended from a leftover Danish prince. His name was Carl, he was a second son, and they sent him to Norway where he took the name Haakon. It was the start of a long royal story followed mostly by the weekly Norwegian supermarket tabloids.

Danes used to see Norwegians as non-threatening, kind of cute. Colorful mountain people with a pleasing, musical dialect, sort of like the English see the Scots.

THE LITTLE BROTHER IS NOW RICH

But over the past thirty years, Norway has become rich, possibly the richest country in the world, because of North Sea Oil. Denmark has to worry about how it will finance its welfare state in the future. Norway doesn't.

Some Danes feel that oil should have been Danish oil. During a meeting to divide up the waters between the two countries in 1963, the Danish negotiator Per Haakerup was photographed with a glass of whisky in his hand.

The rumor was, he was drunk during the meeting and good-naturedly gave up the Ekofisk oilfield, which has since earned Norway billions of dollars.

For the rest of his life, he denied being drunk. His family has actually hired historians to dispel the rumor. And the truth is that at the time, no one even knew about the oil. They thought they were dividing fishing grounds.

But a lot of Danes still believe this story. They believe that some of Norway's money should have been theirs. Envy.

Some Norwegians may believe it, too. There's an urban legend that there's a secret room in the Norwegian National Museum in Oslo that holds the empty bottle of Johnny Walker whisky that maybe, just maybe, made Norway rich.

STORIES OF A SALTY

ON RETURNING TO DENMARK AFTER A VACATION

I 've been out of Denmark for a couple weeks. I've been on vacation in the U.S. But I'm back now, and it only takes a few minutes after I arrive at Kastrup Airport before something happens to destroy the relaxing effect of two weeks off and several thousand kroner spent on transport, hotels, and tasty dinners.

The jolt back to reality usually happens at baggage claim, when one of my fellow fliers bumps right into me at the baggage carousel without saying "*Excuse me*" or "*Pardon*" or "*Entschuldigung,*" or any of those other nice oops-I've-just-run-into-you phrases so common in the rest of the world. For Danes, the standard response after accidentally running into someone is a sullen grunt – HUMPH – along with a sour look of annoyance that you got in their way.

And if I don't get bumped into at the airport, there's bound to be a letter from the tax department waiting when I get home. If it's not the Danish tax department, it's the American tax department, as it was this time. I came home from my relaxing vacation to a completely nonsensical letter from the IRS, written by a machine, sent for some reason in duplicate, asking for six hundred dollars.

But that's what it's like when you have a foot in two different countries. Not just two sets of taxes and tax bureaucrats, but two driver's licenses and two sets of eyeglass prescriptions, since one country won't accept the other's. In each country, I have two sets of pensions: public and private. That means four pension plans, and I basically don't understand any of them.

What's most alarming is when you can see your home country slipping out of focus and Denmark starting to feel like home. When you go back to your country of origin, it can be alarming to realize how Danish you are becoming.

I remember when I first came to Denmark, I thought, "Their cars are so small. How cute!" Now, when I'm in the U.S., I think, "Why do they need such big cars?"

BECOMING A DUAL CITIZEN

Denmark began allowing dual citizenships in 2015, and I was one of the first to apply. This required a language test – including a spoken-word test that required me to create a story around a cartoon image of a lady running to catch a bus. I made up a long and involved story about her troubled love affair with the bus driver. That seemed to satisfy (and interest) the team of examiners.

I also had to take a written test about the various aspects of the Danish government and economy, for which I studied a hefty document about information about shipping and agriculture. Almost none of that was on the test, which was an easy set of questions like, "Is it free to borrow books from the library in Denmark?"

(Shortly after, a less immigrant-friendly government was elected, and my test was replaced with extraordinarily difficult questions like, "When was composer Carl Nielsen born?"

Many native-born Danes complained that they were unable to answer these questions themselves.)

Finally, having passed both the language and national knowledge tests, I was sent to the Danish police for a comprehensive interview. A tough-looking lady who apparently no longer had the stomach for outdoor police work spent an hour questioning me on every aspect of my life, including the kindergarten I attended when I was four. When she was done, she presented me with a typed-out version of everything I had said. I had to sign at the bottom.

That document is now public record; anybody who really wants to can examine it up until my citizenship application goes before the Danish parliament this spring. Every new citizen has to be approved by the Danish parliament, although they usually do this in batches of 100 or so.

NOW I AM A SALTY

I look forward to dual citizenship. Instead of trying to remember where I put my passport, now I can try to remember where I put two passports.

And it seems I've become a salty.

Salty – or *soutpiel* – is an old South African expression. It was a way the white Afrikaans speakers, who were dedicated to South Africa, referred to the white English speakers, who they said had one foot in South Africa and one foot in the UK. This meant that their personal bits were dipped in salt water.

I've got one foot in Denmark and one foot in the U.S., which I suppose makes me a salty, too.

ABOUT THE AUTHOR

Kay Xander Mellish grew up in Wauwatosa, Wisconsin. She graduated *magna cum laude* from New York University, where she studied journalism and art history. After working as a journalist in Berlin, Hong Kong and New York, Kay moved to Copenhagen.

She has worked in the communications departments of Danske Bank and Carlsberg and now runs KXMGroup, a consultancy that helps Danish companies communicate in English.

Kay is also the author of *How to Work in Denmark* (2018) and *Top 35 Mistakes Danes Make in English* (2016).

She is a popular public speaker for both Danish and international audiences and has delivered her "Welcome to Denmark" and "The How to Live in Denmark Game Show" presentations to schools and companies all over Denmark.

Contact Kay via her website at howtoliveindenmark.com.